Looking for Esperanza

Looking
for

Esperanza

THE STORY OF A MOTHER, A CHILD LOST,
AND WHY THEY MATTER TO US

Adriana Páramo

2012 · BENU PRESS, HOPKINS MN

12 13 14 15 16   7 6 5 4 3 2 1   FIRST EDITION

Paperback edition and electronic edition

Printed in the United States

Author photo by Tom Macklin
Cover art and book design by Claudia Carlson,
www.claudiagraphics.com

Text set in Garamond Premiere Pro

ISBN: 978-0-9844629-8-8 (paperback)

ISBN: 978-0-9844629-9-5 (hardcover)

ISBN: 978-0-9844629-5-7 (ebook)

Library of Congress Control Number: 2012940543

P.O. Box 5330
Hopkins, Minnesota 55343-9998
www.benupress.com

Contents

Acknowledgements

Thank you to the women I met while I was looking for Esperanza, for their courage, their candor and their willingness to have their stories told in this book.

Gracias Laura, Griselda, Paulina, Francisca, Cristina, Rosa y por supuesto Esperanza Vasquez. Sin usted, Esperanza, este libro no existiría.

A sincere thank you to Dinty Moore for judging this book worthy of the Social Justice and Equality Award in creative nonfiction and to Benu Press for making its publication possible.

My deep thanks to my creative nonfiction workshop peers at the University of South Florida for their feedback on sections of the original draft of this manuscript.

This book would not exist without John Lantigua, journalist and author, whose article about Esperanza appeared in *The Palm Beach Post* and inspired me to pursue this journey across the Florida fields.

The author gratefully acknowledges the editors who published excerpts from this book.

"Laura" originally appeared as "Looking for Esperanza" in *CONSEQUENCE Magazine*, Spring 2012.

"The ABC of Immigration" originally appeared in *Concho River Review*, Spring 2012.

"The Wetbacks are Coming" originally appeared in *580 Split*, Spring 2012.

"Francisca" originally appeared as "The Limbless Boy of a Mayan Mother," in *The Carolina Quarterly*, Winter 2011.

A synopsis of the book originally appeared as "Looking for Esperanza" in *Magnolia Journal*, Spring 2011.

Adriana Paramo would like to recognize the following agencies for their assistance in her search for Esperanza.

The Coalition of Immokalee Workers • Migrant Farm Worker Justice Project • Healthy Start Coalition of Manatee County, Inc. • Gulf Coast Legal Services, Inc. • Beth-El Farmworker Mission • Florida Association of Community Health Centers • Florida Rural Legal Services • Grassroots Farmworkers Self-Help • Hispanic Council • East Coast Migrant Head Start • RedLands Christian Migrant Association • The Spring of Tampa Bay (Domestic Violence Service Provider) • A.M.A (Alliance of Active Women, Alianza de Mujeres Activas) • Farmworker Association of Florida, Inc. • Guadalupe Social Services, Immokalee • Catholic Charities Dover Migrant Camp • Legislative Comisión on Migrant and Seasonal Labor • Florida Immigrant Advocacy Center

*"Our lives begin to end
the day we become silent about
things that matter."*

— MARTIN LUTHER KING, JR.

*To Esperanza
because her name represents
that universal feeling which
unifies all immigrants: Hope.*

To the memory of her little girl.

Prologue

A few years ago, I read in a Florida newspaper the story of a Mexican woman who crossed the border to the United States on foot. Esperanza left Mexico with four children, but arrived in the USA with three. Her youngest succumbed to dehydration halfway through their desert journey. Esperanza refused to leave her little girl behind; instead, she strapped the body of her dead baby to her own body and, without shedding a tear, continued the journey in mournful silence.

I read the article again and again. I read it with sadness, with anger, with pain, with curiosity, with compassion. Then I read it once more, until the image of this woman trying to smuggle her dead baby into the USA became a mental tattoo. A picture so real in my mind that a part of me began to feel that I knew her, that I had been with her in the desert bearing witness to her baby's death, that it was a matter of time before we would be reunited.

The other part of me understood that the only way to make sense of the ordeal described in the newspaper was to find her. The article said that Esperanza did agricultural work and was living in a trailer park somewhere in Lakeland, the same small city where I lived. I interpreted this as an omen. So far, the other Hispanics I had seen in Lakeland were successful immigrants who drove SUVs, played golf, attended functions at the yacht club and lived the American dream. Esperanza was not one of them.

I took it upon myself to find her and her story.

Initially I looked for Esperanza because she was a woman like me, an immigrant like me, a mother like me. But as an anthropologist, I also wondered about Hispanic women working in the fields as a subculture within the subculture of farmworkers. Was Esperanza's tragedy an exception to the rule? Or is tragedy the rule?

And that's how it all started. My search took me to vegetable fields, citrus groves, ferneries, and packing houses across Florida. It sucked me into an underground subculture of hungry undocumented women, a hidden world of wage slaves, a microcosm of false names, false Social Security numbers, and false hopes.

I went from town to town, from crop to crop, from trailer park to trailer park across Florida, finding different Esperanzas: a Latina who was battered; a Latina who was raped; an illiterate Latina who signed with a cross; a Latina convinced that respect in this country is a privilege of white Americans and will never ask for help; a Latina in jail because she was caught driving without a driver's license; a Latina spiritually and physically broken by a system that failed her; an indigenous woman who doesn't speak either English or Spanish and lived a deaf and mute existence.

In Plant City, instead of Esperanza I met Laura, who, bent at the waist over the strawberry rows, told me how her husband's family had been forced into slavery at a farm nearby.

I went to Immokalee—a Southwestern Florida town that looks like Tijuana. It is a community of forgotten farmworkers who turned whole neighborhoods into little Mexican enclaves marked by poverty and substandard living conditions. There I found Paulina, who told me about her perilous crossings into the USA. All six of them. She walked the desert, swam the river, dug tunnels, crawled under barbed wire—sometimes alone, sometimes with her children. She risked it all to be here.

I looked for Esperanza in a tomato warehouse in Dover where I worked along with other women at the conveyor sorting millions of tomatoes. No, they didn't know about the woman I was looking for, but they knew about three women who waded in pesticides while picking tomatoes and gave birth to deformed babies. The first baby was missing all four limbs. The second baby had an underdeveloped jaw—he choked every time his tongue fell into his throat. The third was born with no visible sexual organs and died of massive birth defects.

Slowly, a hidden Florida began to unravel.

By the time I found her, Esperanza had put me face-to-face not with the shiny state that glimmers on vacationing brochures, but with a wealthy state that treats its farmworkers like meat scraps on the cutting board of bountiful Florida.

Esperanza means Hope in English. I collected the stories of the women I met while I was "Looking for Esperanza," which is to say, looking for Hope. These are women in limbo; their only excess is their poverty; their only possession is their version of the American dream.

The Beginning

It's September. The beginning of the harvest season. The farming communities are starting to come out of their aestivation. During the summer months most farmworkers migrate north looking for jobs. Their neighborhoods become ghost towns. Now that the sun is kinder and the humidity is abating, the houses take on elastic properties, expanding to shelter those who stayed put during the summer, those returning from the harvest in the Northern states, and the newcomers.

As the cooler autumn wind begins to blow across Florida, the farmworkers scout their surroundings looking for affordable shelter. They don't look for anything special; for them, the inadequate is the norm. Any roof becomes home. And so they live in ghettos on the other side of imaginary boundaries that no white man or woman would dare to cross without a Bible, a baseball bat, or a badge.

"Do you know a woman named Esperanza Vasquez?" I ask wherever I go. Only a stranger could ask such an absurd question. The USA is a place where immigrants re-invent themselves, where they adopt different names, carry passports that belong to someone else and use Social Security numbers of deceased people. My question is more often than not met with a blank stare.

I'm looking for Esperanza Vasquez. I make inquiries in the mute underworld of run-down trailer parks where undocumented immigrants live, in those sad agricultural colonies that sprout in unwanted patches of land, away from the locals, away from highways, away from the law and tourists. I look for her in flophouses, dusty bends and abandoned turns kissing the rich Floridian soil from the edges of its wealth like a deprived lover.

"She lost a baby crossing the desert. Any ideas?" I insist. More blank stares. Desert crossing is taboo. Nobody talks about it. It's too painful. It's nobody's business. They don't tell each other what they already know.

"The name rings the bell," a woman told me during a visit to a fernery in Apopka. "Yes, Esperanza. What's her last name?" she asked me as she cut the ferns with one hand and arranged them in bundles with the other.

"Vasquez."

"Vasquez what?" she asked and I realized that I only knew one of her two last names. Hispanics have two last names: father's followed by mother's.

"I'm not sure."

"You're not sure or you don't know?"

"I'm afraid I don't know," I said.

She shot me a look filled with distrust.

"What does she look like?"

"I wish I knew," I said. The woman shook her head and hurried to fasten the bundle of ferns with a rubber band.

"If you're looking for a ghost, you're on your own," she told me. I heard snap, snap as she moved down the row, away from me and my questions.

The rumor is that Esperanza is living somewhere on Hamilton Road, a desolate stretch of nothingness a stone's throw away from Linder Lakeland airport. Hamilton Road is not just a road, it's a blade that silently cuts a ghost town into two rows. Left and right, dilapidated trailers, some without numbers, compete for space along a few hundred weary yards of asphalt, trashed cars, abandoned toys, oxidized bicycles, and statues of the Guadalupe Virgin.

The community is deserted from four a.m. to dusk, when men and women, mostly undocumented Mexicans, are at the local farms planting strawberries or plowing the fields. Their children are either at school, in the care of untrained, unlicensed babysitters, locked inside their houses, or at the field with their parents.

I go back at twilight when I'm more likely to run into a human being. I go through my routine asking about Esperanza, only to hear from a neighbor that she no longer lives on Hamilton Road. She and her children moved into a trailer on Gallatin Street, another in-between-the-toes corner of Lakeland.

Entering the trailer park on Gallatin Street at dusk is like entering a refugee camp. Like being transported to the Third World shantytowns that on TV appear so far away from the America I know. No one would look at this place and say, *Yeah, that's the sunshine state.* No one would think that this brown-faced, short bodied, straight-haired crowd dressed in dirty clothes, looking spirit-broken after fifteen hours in the fields, who don't expect much, don't ask for much, and never receive much, are our neighbors. My neighbors. No one would suspect that a short drive away there are swanky gated communities, an array of eighteen-hole golf courses, spas, boutiques, theaters and every commodity a disposable income can buy.

I look for a friendly face. I find none. Mothers come out of their trailers and call their children in, then close their doors behind them. I feel their curious eyes on me, studying me from behind drawn curtains. I park my car and come out to make myself visible. To let those curious eyes assess this dangerous stranger. Height: 5'5". Weight: 120 pounds. Age: late thirties. Skin color: dark. Ethnicity: *Hispana*. I'm sure I look like one of them until I catch my own reflection in a window. I'm standing next to my sports car: a flashy orange sunset Firebird. In my French-manicured hand, I'm holding one expensive briefcase, handmade, one hundred percent genuine leather. And I'm clean, and well-fed, and healthy. No wonder nobody talks to me. I go back into my car and drive home, that waterfront three-story house in the cul-de-sac of an exclusive gated community where I'm the darkest homeowner my neighbors have ever had. I trade my briefcase for a backpack and my sports car for my husband's truck.

I knock on the trailer where Esperanza supposedly lives. No answer. I walk around peering in through windows and cracks. I can't see any activity. I bang on the sides of the rusted trailer. Nothing. I sit on its wooden steps and wonder if I have what it takes to find Esperanza. I have been looking for her for four months now. Four scorching hot Florida summer months.

The afternoon downpour has carved the dusty ground with gullies. Three barefoot children play in puddles of stagnant rain. They sit on the ground with the muddy water up to their waists and play with a naked toy soldier with a fractured skull. A cloud of black flies hovers over their heads. Nothing seems to matter to them, neither the stench from a nearby heap of garbage that hasn't been collected in weeks nor the flies feeding on the soft mucus dripping from their noses.

"*Hola*," I greet them. They keep on playing as if they haven't heard me.

"You guys know who lives here?" I ask them, pointing over my shoulder at the trailer behind me. They don't answer. They have already learned that a stranger in a trailer park is nothing but trouble. Police come to take grown-ups to jail, Social Services comes to remove children from their families, *la migra*, Immigration, never comes, but if it did, it would be to send the whole family back to the hunger of their native land. It's best not to talk to strangers. They're nothing but trouble.

The twilight sky has morphed into a black cloak, and the children go inside a trailer across the street. I follow them as they splash each other with the stagnant water of muddy puddles. I ask them to call their mom. She is bound to know whether Esperanza is her neighbor.

The trailer is dark inside; only a couple of sixty-watt bulbs hang at the end of bare wires, one in the middle of the living room and one in the kitchen. Between the two rooms, a hole on the floor has been covered with pieces of loose cardboard that I'm sure shift every time they are walked on. A couple of minutes later a woman comes to greet me at the door.

"*Mande*?" A woman, too young to be the mother of three children and too alive to be living in such a sad place stands by the door, wiping her hands on her blue jeans.

"*Buenas*. I'm looking for Esperanza Vasquez. Do you know if she lives here?" I ask her, pointing at the trailer across the street.

"That one's been empty for quite a while." She yawns with a wide-open mouth that exposes a row of decayed molars and a white tongue. "That one's condemned. You know condemned?" I nod and ask her why the trailer has been condemned.

"It was all rotten underneath. Rats were nesting in little holes here and there." Her fingers do a quick trot in the air.

"Then the toilet started to back up. *Ay Virgencita!* The stench. You could smell the shit from the farms." She holds her sunburned face with both hands. "We had to walk around like this," she says, pinching shut her wide nostrils with two fingers.

"One day, a health inspector came and pinned notes on the four sides of the trailer saying that nobody could live there. Do you know the landlord? He's a gringo. You know him?" she asks. I say "No," and she proceeds, "*El blanco*, the white man, shook hands with the inspector and told him he'd fix the problem in no time at all."

She now has a hand on each side of her round hips. "Fix the problem? No, *señor*. Two weeks later a family moved in."

"Esperanza Vasquez and her children?" I ask.

"*Sí, señora*, Esperanza Vasquez."

My heart skips a couple of beats at the sound of the news. After months of looking for her, this is the closest I have been to finding her.

"Esperanza moved into a condemned trailer?"

"*Sí, señora*. And the landlord, you know, El Blanco, told her that if she paid for the repairs, he'd let her and her children live there."

"Free of charge?"

"Free? Nothing's free around here," she says with hands crossed over her protruding belly. "She was homeless, so the gringo told her that if she fixed the trailer, she could live there. For a fee. Of course. $600 a month in case you're wondering."

And so the story goes. Esperanza and her children moved into a rat-infested, condemned trailer, its floor caked with inch-thick blotches of human waste. When the thick Florida sun burnt the floor through the open doors and windows of the trailer, the waste hardened and cracked at random, giving the place a western Badland appearance.

"Thank God the sun was strong that summer. It dried everything up and the stench disappeared like this," she says snapping her fingers.

But as the hurricane season crept into the summer months, bringing damp winds and downpours, the floor of the trailer acquired a gelatinous consistency of putrid excrement and dead flies. The neighbors collected plastic bags and handed them to Esperanza. She organized them in bunches that she nailed to the door. Esperanza taught her children to snatch bags every time they entered the trailer, slip it over their shoes and fasten it around their ankles with a rubber band. "You understand?" the woman asks me. "So they didn't get shit in their shoes."

For two months Esperanza dodged and outsmarted the landlord. Sometimes at the sight of the landlord's car she'd run around the trailer switching the lights off, ordering her children to be quiet. She'd wait in the dark, weary and dry-mouthed, until the landlord got tired of knocking on her door and left with sore knuckles. By the third month, the landlord and his brother, a ruthless cowboy just out of the county jail, were paying Esperanza two visits a day. Sometimes three.

"And one day, they just ran into each other around the corner. Bang!" she says stopping her open right hand just a mere inch away from her nose. "He told her to either fix the trailer or leave. He was risking getting fined and if he had to pay so much as one dollar in fines, he'd tell the police that she was a squatting wetback and get her deported."

Deportation was the magic word. The word that set Esperanza's heart into panic, so violent and so loud that it kept her awake for nights in permanent vigil, devising solutions, each more outrageous than the last. One morning she went around knocking on everyone's trailer, borrowing shovels and buckets. She collected every sharp tool she could get her hands on, went inside her trailer, scraped the floor with the edges of the shovels, trowels and hoes and proceeded to pack crusts of soft waste in plastic bags. She dug a hole in a piece of land behind her trailer and proceeded to bury the bags. When they were done, she and her children went back inside, covered their mouths with old rags and the sleeves of sweaters and on all fours they scrubbed the floor clean with Clorox until the stench of feces morphed into the stink of bleach. She went to the local flea market and bought a secondhand rug. It was black and beige and had a red dragon in the middle with Chinese writing on the sides. She liked it. It was cheerful and big enough to cover the holes in the kitchen floor. She bought rat poison and spread it all over under the trailer. Problem solved. For seventy two hours, she didn't dread the landlord, who never came. The rat poison started to work its magic and Esperanza collected an army of dead rodents every day. Unfortunately, many of the rats died under the trailer in hidden grooves that she couldn't access. Three days later, the reek of bleach had been overpowered by the repugnant odor of rapidly decomposing rats trapped in the pipes.

"Poor Esperanza had to call a plumber. You know how much he said the repairs would cost?" she asks but doesn't wait for my answer. "1200 dollars. Imagine that," she says. "I told her to run away in the middle of the night. How in the world was she going to pay such a fortune only to fix somebody else's property?"

Esperanza heeded her neighbor's advice. One day at around two a.m., she packed everything she had, loaded it onto the bed of a borrowed pickup, and left with her children. She didn't say goodbye to anyone. Not even her neighbor.

"Do you know where she moved to?" I ask.

The young woman takes a good look at me from head to toe as if trying to ascertain the kind of person I am. She suddenly realizes she has broken the unwritten code of silence. She has given too much information about one of her own to a stranger.

"Who are you anyway? Are you from her church or from the Hispanic Council?"

I nod to both sheepishly and introduce myself. She extends her callous hand and mumbles her name.

"Sorry, did you say Olivia?"

"Oh call me anything you want. Olivia will do."

They are skittish with names; their given names don't match the ones on their Social Security cards. They are Olivia, Maria, Rosario, anything but themselves.

"Where did you say Esperanza is?" I ask.

"I didn't tell you nothing," she says, suddenly annoyed.

I wonder who she really is, why she came to the USA, what powerful dreams compelled her to cross a raging river in an inner tube or trek across the treacherous desert. I want to ask her about the deep scar on her chin and that bruise on her forearm that looks like a purple cloud. I want to know if I could come back some other day and interview her properly, tape recorder and all.

"Tape recorder?" she asks, waving her index fingers in the air and making loud tsk, tsk noises with her yellow teeth. "I thought you were from the church," she says.

I try to explain that I'm not actually from the church but that I mean no harm. That I'm not with *la migra* either and that she's safe with me. That I'm just a writer, a collector of stories. To no avail. The more I try to explain myself the more suspicious she becomes. She starts closing the door to her trailer, slowly; she asks me to leave, gently; she tells me I ask too many funny questions, seriously. Before she closes the door completely, one of her children wraps his thin arms around her legs, rubs his sleepy eyes with one dirty fist. "I'm hungry," he says. Then she closes the door all the way.

Paulina

It's still hot. Florida is throbbing with large flocks of tourists in the theme parks around Orlando and the many resort cities that rim the coasts. Approximately seventy-six million tourists visited Florida last year and spent nearly fifty-seven billion dollars, but as I drive off the interstate and along State Road 27, I wonder if a single penny of this money or of the nine billion dollars generated by the citrus industry has ever touched the Hispanic communities that I drive across. On my way to Immokalee, where I've been told I can find Esperanza, I drive in and out of towns such as Frostproof, Sebring, Lake Placid, Venus, Palmdale, La Belle and Felda, all cluttered with small enclaves of ramshackle Hispanic farmworking communities.

The one I'm looking for in Immokalee is located across the street from a McDonald's. I stand underneath the tarnished yellow M, a sad arch in desperate need of pressure washing. The trailer park is a group of crowded cheek-by-jowl rectangular boxes surrounded by broken-down cars, garbage blowing in the hot breeze, and dying dogs lurking under porches. I've been driving for hours; the sun, the sadness of the towns along the way, some of which I visited at the beginning of the summer, and the fading of my hope of finding Esperanza are wearing me down. I'm beginning to wonder if I'll ever find her.

I knock on the door of trailer number 42. The aluminum is moldy and hot to the touch. A tawny woman in her late twenties comes out of the trailer. She's got slanted eyes full of mischief and a derisive grin across her sweaty face. She looks me up and down and jerks her head upward as if saying, what's up? I inquire about Esperanza. No, she doesn't know anyone by that name.

"What do you want her for? Does she owe you money or is she fooling around with your man?" she asks and winks with one eye then the other.

"I'm a writer," I say.

"What's that?"

"I write books."

"Books? Her cheeks flutter like she is about to burst into laughter. I nod.

"The only book I've ever held in my hands was a phone book," she says as she falls into a raucous fit of laughter that makes her eyes disappear into their sockets. There is a stubborn exuberance about her, a flare of self-assertiveness that I haven't seen in any of the other women I have talked to so far.

"I write stories about women working in the fields," I explain. "That's why I'm looking for Esperanza. She has a good story that I would like to write about."

"Well, well. If you're looking for stories, you're in the right place. I'm Paulina," she says as she offers me a thin, damp hand and gently pulls me into her trailer. Inside, everything is dark and hot and humid. Everything sad, everything broken. I accidentally kick a naked Barbie doll lying on the floor; she is missing two limbs. We walk by a black and white TV set placed on a Coca Cola crate; its screen is cracked. I wonder if it works. We sit on what is left of a couch with torn cushions and stained armrests. Paulina points at a small air conditioning unit dangling off a hole in a sidewall of the trailer.

"Doesn't work," she says. "I use a Mexican A/C system," she adds as she removes a piece of cardboard covering a broken window. The heat is stifling. I ask her if we could talk outside; she says no, it's too hot, she's been outdoors all day, the last thing she wants to see is the sun.

Paulina grew up on a corn farm in the Mexican state of Oaxaca. They weren't wealthy but the corn that her father's small piece of land produced was enough to feed a family of nine, seven children and two parents. It was during the nineties, when she was fourteen, that their situation moved rapidly from acceptable to tough to unsustainable. Something bad was happening in the corn industry, although Paulina is not sure what it was. Something to do with her father not being able to compete against cheaper corn imported from the USA. By then, NAFTA had already taken effect; imports of corn to Mexico from the United States increased nearly twenty-fold, plunging small farmers like Paulina's father into absolute poverty.

Her father moved his family farther and farther up Oaxaca's mountainsides as he strove to diversify his crops and forget about corn. But he failed, the children went hungry, and Paulina was sent to live with Rogelio, a man she had never seen before, the son of a wealthy family of Oaxacan ranchers who was only too happy to take up a young bride.

Two weeks later, the young man paid Paulina's father a visit. He wanted to return Paulina the following day. There was no point in having a woman if the woman didn't let her man touch her. If every time he wanted to show her some *love*, she squealed like a pig, scratching, kicking, biting and spitting in his face. The deal was off.

Paulina stops, clears her throat, takes a deep breath and asks me if I have a father. She doesn't give me time to say no.

"I don't know what yours would've done but I'll tell you what mine did," she says. "I know this because Rogelio told me."

Her father stood tall in front of Rogelio, his thumbs tucked under the enormous eagle on the belt buckle. "It's not my fault that you're not man enough," the father said sucking his teeth between words. They argued some more, drank gourds of homebrewed *mezcal*, and had a long man-to-man discussion about women during which the verbs *to love* and *to fuck* were used interchangeably.

"It's not my fault if you're a *pinche joto*, a damn faggot," the father said. "If you're a real man, behave like one. Who's the man of the house? Huh? You or Paulina?" The father prodded, hissing his words, spewing poison into the air. Rogelio listened, his eyes cast down, his head nodding in agreement with the old man. "If you don't behave like a real man, I'll start thinking that you're a *joto*, and which woman in Oaxaca will want to marry a *pinche joto,* huh? We men don't beg women for love, *hijo.* If God put Paulina in your bed, it's because it's for you to take, not to for you to come here crying like a little girl. You know what I mean?" Paulina's father gave his own crotch a firm squeeze.

By the time the old man had said his last word, Rogelio knew exactly what to do. He drove his truck home, train whistles going off in his head, his manhood bulging under his blue jeans. It was midnight when Rogelio woke Paulina up. He grabbed her by her hair, forced his tongue into her mouth and pinned her against the mattress with his own weight. She punched and kicked and spat. Rogelio ripped the white cotton of her pajamas, spread her legs with his right knee and entered her. Eight months and two weeks after the attack, a baby boy was born. Paulina was fifteen.

And that was how a treaty signed thousands of miles away from Oaxaca turned up being the pact that sealed the destinies of thousands of women who left Tuxtepec, Ixtlan, Juchitan, Tehuantepec, and Huatulco, among others, and made their way North to feed off the same hand that had displaced them in the first place: the American economy.

Paulina's oldest brother was the first one in the family to cross the border. He got tired of waiting for the situation to improve in Oaxaca, for the price of corn to go back up again; he got tired of not having a future, of being hungry and penniless. He took the risk, crossed the border, and found a job in Florida. The few dollars he wired to his parents were enough proof, to everyone in town, of his success. Enough to entice Paulina to follow his steps; she'd leave her toddler with her parents, cross the border, find a job, rent a small room, and live a Rogelio-free life.

Her brother told her where to find a human smuggler, a *coyote, pollero,* or *patero.* He'd lead her from Oaxaca all the way to Phoenix and then to Immokalee, Florida, where there was money for anyone, with or without papers, willing to work hard. No questions asked.

"I'm going to take a piss," Paulina says abruptly and disappears down the hallway.

I scribble notes off to the side about the Coyote mythlore among Native Americans. In creation myths, Coyote appears as the Creator himself. He took up a handful of mud and out of it made people. As the culture hero, Coyote's major attributes are transformation and traveling. He changes the ways of rivers, cuts through mountains, creates new landscapes and gets food for people. I wonder about the origin of all the different names for a human smuggler.

"Why are they called coyotes?" I shout at Paulina from the sofa. "You know?"

"No idea," she shouts back from the toilet. "Maybe because they know the desert like jackals do? I don't know."

I hear her trip the handle on the tank to flush the toilet. It makes a metallic sound but I don't hear any water. The bowl must have been empty.

"I know why they're called *polleros,* though," she says as she sits next to me. "Because the wetbacks look like chickens, *pollos,* being herded across the border." But that's not important, she tells me. Those *chingadas* have nothing to do with her story.

"My brother paid the coyote $800 to pick me up in Oaxaca and drop me off in Immokalee. It might not sound like much now, but remember that was a long time ago. It was a whole *chingo* of money because Oaxaca is far away from the border. Did you know that? It's closer to Guatemala than to the crossing."

The coyote led Paulina, another woman, and ten men, all from Oaxaca, first all the way to Nogales, then the 300 miles between Nogales and a place near Phoenix, and lastly from Arizona to southwest Florida where Immokalee is.

"How long did it take you to make it to Immokalee?" I ask Paulina.

She closes her eyes and screws up her face as half of her right index finger disappears into one of her nostrils. She does some serious digging up her nose, pulls the finger out and looks at its tip as if it were the answer to my question.

"The whole trip? I don't remember; maybe three weeks, maybe more. But the *mero* desert? That one I remember: five *chinga* nights and six *chinga* days." Paulina uses the word *chinga* in its broadest scope of meanings. *Chinga* is everything good, everything evil, and everything in between.

I've heard countless border crossing accounts; they take place at night, under the complicity of the darkness and the guidance of the stars.

"You walked at night, right?" I ask Paulina just to confirm.

"At night? No way. The *migra* figured out that the *pollos* walked at night and after dark they were everywhere, like God. The coyote told us that during the day the desert was empty because those gringos are *muy flojos,* wimps, and can't stand the heat of the day. That's why we walked from six a.m. to ten p.m. every day for six days."

Paulina picks her nose once more, wipes her finger sideways on her stained shirt and laughs. "Do you want to know what I did all those nights?" I nod. "I played games with the stars. I would spot one, make a wish and close my eyes again. Then I'd open them once more, spot another one and make a different wish...and like that until I fell asleep."

"What did you wish for?"

"For my life, what do you think? I wished I could make it alive to the USA. After that, I wished for *meras chingadas.* To find a job doing anything decent, save money, bring my boy, buy him a tricycle, toys, clothes. I'm telling you, just *chingadas.*"

It occurs to me that if Paulina could define life in a few words, it would be something in between *re-padre,* very good, and *chingo,* totally screwed up. And how would she describe life in the USA? Probably as a mixture of *tiempos padres,* good times, and *tiempos bien chingados.*

"Did you have enough food and water for the journey?"

"No, not really. Whatever we had packed in Oaxaca, we ate on our way to Sonora. By the time we got to the border we only had crackers, a few cans of beans and some apples." I shake my head while I take notes, but Paulina hurries to finish her story as if to dispel any misunderstandings.

"Don't feel sorry. The desert gives you everything you need to survive, you just have to look. Some trees give you fruits and if you are lucky you can bring down a vulture with a slingshot. They taste like chicken," she says and lets out one of her hearty cackles. "Or you catch a snake, cook it and you make snake burritos." Paulina slaps her thigh and stomps the floor with her right foot. The trailer reverberates a little with her thunderous laugh.

"How about the days when there was no food? How did you cope with hunger?" Her expression turns somber, her humorous face evaporates.

"I lied on the ground like a baby, like this." Paulina adopts a fetal position on the couch. I imagine her now, rolling her body into a ball, pushing with her hands the part of her abdomen where hunger gnaws at her empty entrails. "Or you think about the new life in America and then it's not so bad. The hunger quickly goes away."

"And water? You can't last in the desert without water."

"There is water in the desert. I already told you, you just have to look. If you see cows, for sure for sure, there is water around. It's not your American bottled water; it stinks because it's stagnant water, but hey, if it's good for the cows, it's good for you too, right?"

Paulina was unafraid of being caught and sent back to Mexico. She was seventeen, fearless, determined to leave behind the poverty of Oaxaca. She walked, crouched, crawled, sat, stood, lay low, and ran on command. Her coyote was her master; her life was in his hands. He knew the desert winds as well as he knew the skies. He read the trees, discovered hidden tracks, smelled the water from a distance, spotted helicopters before anyone else. He ran, walked, and crawled along with his human cargo. His life was also at stake, but unlike the lives of the migrants he guided through the desert, his had a price: $9,600 ($800 for each of the twelve border-crossers.)

I've been told that there are good coyotes and bad coyotes. The former risk their lives while they lead and take care of their human cargo; throughout their journey they are guides, companions, fathers, cooks, and even priests. They ensure that the group is delivered on time at a safe place in one of the American bordering states. The latter abandon their passengers in the desert and flee with their money; they team up with desert bandits that assault, rob, and rape; they run away when the border patrol shows up; they promise a bed and a warm meal at the end of the journey but vanish in the middle of the desert night, taking with them everything the migrants have and owe.

"I was in Okeechobee *pizcando* oranges the day after I arrived in Immokalee." Paulina's hands contort in the air as if she was screwing in a thousand bulbs.

"I slept a few hours on a bench in a park, and at four in the morning, I went to a parking lot in downtown Immokalee where my brother told me the *chiveros* came looking for day laborers. There were many men, all *puro* Mexican, and me. I was the only woman. A man came in a beat-up school bus and said, "We're picking oranges in Okeechobee, who's coming?" I jumped on the bus and went to work at the groves. I didn't even know what Okeechobee was. I thought it was a kind of orange." Paulina unscrews more light bulbs and tells me that she picked oranges in Okeechobee and tomatoes in Immokalee for a year until she decided to go back to Oaxaca.

"To see my parents and *mi chamaquito,* my boy."

Little did Paulina know as she bought a bus ticket to Mexico that her return to the USA would be plagued with obstacles, blisters, and border patrol officers.

The next time I come to Immokalee to see Paulina, another woman opens the door of trailer number 42. She looks younger than Paulina, but her eyes tell me that she is about to buckle from some colossal weight. She's Simona, Paulina's youngest sister. She holds the door ajar and covers the right side of her face with a strand of ebony, sparkly hair. The strand is not long enough to cover what she wants to hide: a black crescent outlining the sharp edge of her right eye socket. It takes me a while to notice how beautiful she is: her perfectly straight nose, the pointy chin that gives her an air of dignity, her oblique sad brown eyes, the black straight bangs on each side of her forehead; it all fades into insignificance before the dark half-moon under her right eye that I can't ignore.

She lets me in and while we wait for Paulina, we sit across from each other in silence—I, on the couch, she, on a wobbly plastic chair by the TV—examining each other when we think the other is not looking.

"Do you know a Mexican woman by the name of Esperanza Vasquez?" I ask Simona.

"I'm new here. I don't know anybody," she says, her eyes cast down. I clear my throat and shuffle my feet to get her attention.

"What happened to your eye?" I ask.

She gets up. "I fell and that's all there is to it," she says before disappearing behind a plastic curtain that separates her world from Paulina's.

Paulina's trailer smells of urine and garlic. I sit on a plastic crate by the window but she grabs me by my wrist and tells me to sit on the couch. A crate won't do my bony ass any good, she says, winking and shaking her head. We sit next to each other on the couch and I pull my notebook out of my bag. She has just shampooed her hair; it is wet and it gives off a fruity scent.

"Where were we?" she asks, looking at my notebook.

I read her my last sentence on the page. "You stayed in Oaxaca with your family and your three-year-old son until the money ran out."

Six months later, she joined a group of chickens on their way to the border, this time to Tijuana. Trips from Tijuana are simple, short, and cheap. But they are high risk because the place is always crawling with border patrol agents.

"The coyote told us we'd cross *la linea* through an underground tunnel. Do you know that word? Tunnel?" I say "*sí*" and she proceeds. "I ask because none of us had heard such word. The coyote explained the word several times but we kept asking him: "Are we going to die?" or "Will we be able to breathe?" or "What if the ceiling falls on our heads?" At the end he got fed up repeating himself and said that we were going to have to trust him and when he said the word *órale,* go, we had to run. That's what we did."

On the Mexican side, a few yards away from the border, the coyote showed them the entrance to the tunnel. It was a wood plank door on the ground covered with garbage and empty beer bottles. Once he cleared the door, opened it, and said *órale,* Paulina and her companions ran without looking back. She doesn't remember what the tunnel looked like inside or how long it was; all she remembers is the sound of their frightened feet stomping the ground and the cars going back and forth between the USA and Mexico right above their heads.

After the tunnel, there was nothing but the vast desert. No moon, no stars, no fires, no flashlights. Nothing. For about five hours, they walked in a straight line, one behind the other, hands outstretched in the dark like the blind. Before three a.m., they heard an overhead whirring noise, followed by a ray of light so intense that it occurred to Paulina that it was God talking to them from the very heavens.

"The helicopter chased us around with its searchlight, and we scattered all over the place like scared chickens. Nobody knew what to do, so we ran and screamed and cursed. A few minutes later out of nowhere came a border patrol van. The *bolillos* packed us into the van and drove us back to the border. They didn't say a word, so we didn't talk."

"Did they take your names?"

"No. They *no mas* threw us into the van and didn't open their mouths until we got to the border. Then they opened the door and said in Spanish *váyanse a sus casas,* go home. We hopped out of the van and ran just in case the *bolillos* changed their minds and took us to jail."

They rested all day and that night they made a second attempt at crossing the border with the USA. They'd be led by the same coyote. They stuck to the initial plan: Take the tunnel, walk into the desert, cross the line, wait for the drivers to pick them up at an agreed point, make it to California. The instructions were repeated until everybody understood the rules: If Immigration were to capture them and ask for their names, they'd give out fake names, and nobody, absolutely nobody in the group would reveal the identity of the coyote. They'd say they were traveling together, nobody was guiding them across, otherwise Immigration would take them to jail, take their names, keep the coyote behind bars, and hinder their chances to cross again with him. One coyote behind bars is one less chance to make it to North.

But this time the U.S border patrol officers were waiting for them at the exit of the tunnel, another wood plank door like the entrance. The Mexicans didn't get a chance to scatter, or run, or curse. They were rounded up, and in a few minutes they were back on the patrol car and on their way to the Mexican border.

"After that, our tunnel plan *se chingó. La migra* used the tunnel to catch the few *sonsos* that didn't know the border patrol had already found it. One by one, like dead fish in the water, they crawled out of the tunnel and *la migra* would catch them straight away."

"What happened next?" I ask Paulina.

"Next, everything happened, like pig's fodder. We were caught six times total. Two with the goddamn tunnel plan, two after jumping over the fucking fence, and two crawling underneath it." Paulina cocks her head as if trying to retrieve her memories from one side of her head. Sun rays make their way into the trailer to lick her wide, brown nose. Her whole face glistens with sweat and every time she moves her head, I smell apples and citrus in her hair. If the trailer still reeks of garlic and piss, I don't notice it. Outside the trailer it is ninety degrees.

While she tells me about her six consecutive attempts to cross the border, I steal glances at her. She's chubby with generous rolls of soft flesh around her midsection and breasts that hang lazily over her belly. It's hard to imagine her running, jumping, crawling. Hard to imagine a layer of lean muscle running beneath her soft flesh. But I try. It's important to me to be able to visualize her trapped in a desert moment, caught in the chase, dashing north without ever looking back.

"After the second go, the coyote decided to take us over the fence. By now he was already losing money because we were staying at his house in Tijuana and his wife had been feeding us for two days. You don't give those *cabrones* a penny until you get to the USA. So, if his group is still in Mexico, he's not getting any money. See how it works?"

I see her in an abandoned junkyard. She jumps over an old iron border fence and runs some more. She crouches behind a pile of crushed cars and waits in silence until the coyote says *ándenle pollitos.* She runs as fast as she can, her hands curled into fists, her arms in a mad pendulum swing, back and forth, back and forth. She sees the new fence. Mounted at its top is a mesh of razor barbed wire. She climbs the chain link fence. She steps on someone's fingers. Someone stomps on hers. She prays and curses. She takes one deep final big breath. This is gonna hurt, she thinks. She grabs the razor barbed wire with both hands and swings her body over the fence. Fire serrates her bloody hands. The razors have peeled the flesh off her fingers. She is looking at her bones protruding through a mess of red slicked skin, shining in the night like daggers. Then she hears the dogs. Men speaking in English. She sees the flashlights, people in uniform, the German shepherds. Game over. In minutes, all the scattered immigrants are rounded up and taken to a van.

One of the agents asked her name.

"Selena," Paulina said.

"Last name?"

She was tempted to say Quintanilla-Perez like the queen of Tejano music, but settled for Cruz, just in case the border patrol knew the singer. Two hours later they were back in Mexico.

I stop taking notes. "I'm exhausted just listening to you, Paulina," I say. "Didn't you just feel like quitting?"

"Quitting is for wimps," Paulina says. "I had no option, *doña*. It was either die a slow death in Oaxaca like a starving cow, or die fighting for my son's future."

No, quitting never crossed their minds. They were weary, sleepy, and hungry, and the longer they stayed on the Mexican side of the fence, the more desperate they became to be on American soil. Then it began to rain. The coyote rubbed his hands together. Rain along the fence was good, he said. The drainage canals soften and give way to the spring rain runoff. As soon as the coyote said his magic words, the group was on all fours, scratching the rain-soaked ground with their bare hands, digging a passage beneath the fence. It didn't have to be big, just enough to crawl out of poverty and into the promises of *El Norte*. But they didn't dig fast enough and were captured again.

"Didn't I just send you back home, *Se-le-na?*" the border agent asked Paulina.

"Who? Me? *No señor*, this is my first time." Frustrated and angry, Paulina curled her hands into fists as she said her name for the record, Dolores Jimenez, like the revolution heroine from Aguascalientes.

A new Tijuana morning welcomed back Paulina and her companions. As soon as she opened her eyes, she felt the pain. Her body was sore from running and falling and creeping. Arms and legs crisscrossed with lines of dry blood, her limbs looked like maps of faraway lands. Her body was a mess of scratches, open wounds, blisters, scars—all testaments to her determination to escape hunger. *Chinga la madre que te parió.* Fuck. Fuck. Fuck.

The next day, they tried the fence again. This time, the coyote came armed with a blowtorch to cut the metal grate above a wide drainage tunnel. No sooner had he started to melt the metal than a helicopter shone its searchlights onto the group. It wasn't God talking to them from the very heavens; Paulina knew that much. They scattered, ran, tripped and fell to the ground, cried, prayed and shouted obscenities at everyone and everything. They were sent back. No questions asked.

Paulina shakes her head slowly. She looks tired. I tell her that I can come back another day.

"What, you don't want to know how the hell I ended up in California?"

"Of course, I do," I say.

"The same *chingada*: run like fuck, hide like you've killed your own mother, get wet, then hot, sleep in the desert, under a car, behind a garbage can. I did all that and sure enough I ended up in Fresno, California."

A woman selling *tortillas* spotted Paulina dozing on a bench at a bus station. They exchanged a few words: Hello, how are you? You look like you could use a good *mole Oaxaqueño*. Are you new here? You know who needs a hand? And who can put me up for a little while until I get my life sorted out? And today must be your lucky day because I have an empty mattress in my living room.

Paulina ended up living with *la tortillera*, who not only shared her food and home with Paulina, but also found her a job at a tomato packing house. Finally a roof over her head, a few dollars earned under the table, a form of life with room for new dreams, long-term plans, and who knows, maybe a man. Yes, a man. He'll have to be dark, tall and strong, the way she liked her men. A Mexican stud, young enough to endure the ravaging nightly heat of her bed sheets.

The first time INS showed up at the packing house, everybody ran except Paulina.

"I was just working, minding my own goddamn business. Sorting out the tomatoes those *cabrones* from *la migra* were about to eat in their fancy salads. Why was I going to run? For being on my feet twelve hours a day? Was that a crime? I didn't think so, so I kept working, as if nothing was happening."

The immigration agents rounded up those who ran around the conveyor belt, out of the packing house and into the tomato groves. That time six of her coworkers were taken away. No time for goodbyes, packing, or sorting life out. Everything they had worked for evaporated in less than half an hour. One minute they were working and the next minute they were in custody on their way to jail, then Mexico.

Two months later, Immigration raided the packing house again. This time,

Paulina didn't take risks and she ran, fast and bitter, out of the packing house and into the bushes surrounding the groves. That time, Immigration took away nine coworkers.

"Fifteen in two months," Paulina says. "Then they came again and took some more. That's not a way to work. Working and watching over your shoulder like a criminal? Noooo! After seven months in California I said enough is enough, and I went back to my village in Oaxaca."

By the time Paulina left the USA, she was one month pregnant. The father of the baby, a young man from Piedras Negras, was always on the move: one day on this side of the border, the next day on the other side. He was a traveler, a free-spirited Mexican not ready yet for a home, let alone a family. Paulina stayed in Oaxaca six months.

"*Si, Doña.* I couldn't last any longer. Oaxaca was even worse than last time, poorer, and you know what? Emptier. I think the whole Oaxaca left for *El Norte.* Even Rogelio. His family lost the land and he his fancy truck." Paulina looks both ways over her shoulders. "You know where that ugly dick is now?" she asks, her eyebrows perched up somewhere on her forehead.

"Here in the USA?" I volunteer.

"Nuh-uh, right here in Immokalee. *El cabrón.* Sometimes we run into each other; I look the other way. If he tries to talk to me, I tell him I don't know him."

Six months later, Paulina was on her way to Piedras Negras, where the father of her unborn baby was waiting for her. They had a plan. Cross the border, make it to Dallas where *las maquiladoras* were hiring Mexican women, undocumented or not, and live life the right way—one day at a time.

"I was seven months pregnant when I crossed again."

"It sounds like a dangerous time to attempt crossing," I comment. "How much did you have to pay this time?"

"Nothing. Didn't I tell you the father of my baby was a *pollero?*" Paulina giggles coyly, embarrassed by the boldness of her omission. "I told you before: He was one day here and the next day there. He crossed the Rio Bravo with *pollos.* That was his business."

The Rio Bravo was chest high when it wound its way through Piedras Negras. It was March, a particularly cold March, when Paulina and her coyote decided to cross the river. Paulina took her sandals off and dipped her toes into the water. A wave of goose bumps strolled up her shins and knees and even made the creature inside her belly recoil.

"He said, 'Take off your clothes,' and I said, 'No way, look at my belly. I'm not letting you anywhere near me." Then he explained that if we showed up at the other side of the river soaking wet, people would immediately know we were wetbacks."

Paulina took off her maternity dress. It was ankle-long, white with a thousand tiny blue flowers scattered around the fabric like a garden, with a baby-blue bib and a back tie. It was a secondhand dress she had bought at *la pulga,* a flea market, before she left Fresno.

She had expected a kinder river, one with still waters that wound through solitude and silence, shimmering in the sun like mirrors. But the river was angry that day and the quiet stretches of its flow had morphed into rollicking rapids. This time Paulina was afraid—afraid of hurting the baby she carried, a baby who was not responsible for her decisions. "*Virgen de Guadalupe, Virgen de Guadalupe, Virgencita mia,* protect me and my *chamaquito* from this strong current," she chanted like a spell as she rubbed on her swollen belly. She stood by the raging water in her white nylon slip, the elastic band of her cotton underwear in perfect alignment with her protruding navel.

The coyote put their clothes and shoes in a black garbage bag, blew air into it, sealed it with what he called his "secret *patero* knot," wrapped the bag around his waist with his shoelaces, and whispered a special prayer to Saint Toribio Romo Gonzalez, the protector of all wetbacks.

"Ready?" he asked Paulina.

"Ready," she said, and walked into the water.

The smooth surface of the river rocks felt like wet velvet on the soles of her feet. Paulina slipped once; her right leg wobbled back and forth over a round mossy mound at the bottom of the river. She regained her balance. *Virgencita de Guadalupe.* She slipped again; her knees buckled from the cold and the furious kicks her baby planted on one side of her womb. Paulina tugged at the rim of her coyote's underwear, her knuckles white and bloodless from cold and fear.

"We were in the middle of the river when I lost my balance again. *Ahí fue cuando me llevó la chingada!,* that's when everything went to shit."

She lost her balance and her grip of the coyote's underwear. The current swallowed her whole. It dragged her downriver. It tossed her and her baby around like a discarded babushka. Streams of water flooded her nostrils. Her hands clasped fistfuls of air and water, air and water, then only water. She heard a gurgle. Everything went black. She heard nothing else.

When Paulina came to, she was on the American side of the river. Her dark brown-eyed coyote with the golden tooth was looking at her. "You almost got us killed," he told her. He wasn't tall, but he had a delicious Coahuilan smile, which in the midst of her confusion she had the courage to hope her baby inherited.

For six weeks, Paulina called home the back of a *maquiladora* in Dallas. During the day, she folded and hung shirts ready to be shipped to an unknown place. The shirts were exported who knows where, Paulina says, with a label that read "Made in the USA," despite their being made by undocumented Mexicans breaking American laws. During the night, Paulina and a group of co-workers slept in the back of the factory in a large hall furnished with bunk beds, military style. They wouldn't allow her to live there with her baby. Paulina packed and left for Immokalee again.

"I arrived in Immokalee, and within hours I was already *pizcando* tomatoes," she says. There is so much pride in her voice, such deep sense of accomplishment, that right at this moment I feel happy for her.

"You must have been ready to give birth," I comment. "That's dangerous."

"Why dangerous? I don't pick tomatoes with my belly." Paulina's chest throbs with laughter. She taps my knee with a cupped hand. "I was pregnant, not sick. You can be pregnant and work at the same time, you know."

In Immokalee, Paulina went to live at the *frenchy house,* The Friendship House, a place that offers warm meals and shelter to the homeless. "That's some place," she tells me. A pang of nostalgia creeps in between her words. "They treated me so well. Like they were my family. Like I was important or something. I would have liked to stay there for the rest of my life."

It was at the Friendship House where she gave birth to a baby girl.

"Where was your man all this time?"

"My man?"

"Yes, the father of your girl."

"That's the father of my girl, not my man. And Rogelio? The other *cabrón*? He was the father of my boy. But I have no man. Nuh-uh."

Three months after the birth of her baby girl, Paulina heard the news. Her coyote from the state of Coahuila was in a Texan jail. The border patrol captured him and the twenty-two *pollos* he was smuggling into the USA from his beloved Piedras Negras.

"Did you visit him in jail?"

"Did I visit him? *Doña,* I had just given birth to his baby. Of course I went. And you want to know the little present life had for me there?"

More head cocking, more smirking, more tsk-tsking. I brace for another surprise.

"I found out that this *cabrón* was married and had five children. His wife came to visit him the very same day I went to show him his baby girl. So when he told me that he was going to be in jail for two years, and that he was going to miss me, and that he was going to look for me and take me to live with him when he was free, I just gave him a piece of my mind. *Perro chingalamala!* I told him, I hope you rot in jail. I hope you catch tuberculosis or leprosy and become a stinky mess of oozing sores. I hope you get the crabs and your dick falls off."

Human trafficking across the border requires precision, planning, good communication between all the parties, and a budget, because in this business, everybody takes a piece of the pie. And the pie is big. The coyote leads the group to a pre-arranged location in Arizona where they are met by one or more *raiteros,* rides. The *raitero* drives the group to a safe house in Phoenix. From there, phone calls are made to the relatives of the immigrants, who are instructed to wire money to a specific Western Union office. Once the money has been wired, the same or a different *raitero* drives the group across the USA to their final destinations.

What if no money is wired? What if the immigrants' contacts cannot pay the coyote's fees? A different arrangement has to be made; after all, human trafficking is a money-making business and no coyote would risk his life to smuggle a human cargo in exchange for nothing. Whenever money can't be obtained from the immigrant's contacts, the coyote might have to take those people back to Mexico. But more often than not, he "sells" his cargo to a crew leader or contractor.

The contractor works for an American farmer who gladly turns a blind eye to the situation. The farmer washes his hands by having a front man directly dealing with the workers. The farmer doesn't speak Spanish, nor does he want to. He pays his contractor a fixed fee for specific agricultural tasks and walks away from the situation he had created by leaving the lives of his own workers in the hands of a greedy contractor.

Good coyotes never work alone. They have a solid network of drivers, co-coyotes, safe-house keepers, and, of course, crew leaders out in the farms. The crew leaders or contractors are in charge of squeezing the debt money out of immigrants. The duration of this labor bondage is as arbitrary as it is criminal and varies from six months to two years, depending on the amount owed and the crew leader's caprice.

It's December. At dawn when Florida is still asleep, a veil of icy air descends onto the fields. Before Floridians wake up, icicles hang lazily from the branches of oak trees, like sloths. A freezing cloud of fog hovers over the tomato groves, the bean fields, the orange trees. Thousands of Hispanic workers brave the four a.m. cold when they start their journey to the various crops. They wear woolly hats and mismatched gloves, ripped leggings underneath their blue jeans, fleece jackets, layers of promotional t-shirts, and two pairs of socks. In parking lots flanking agricultural communities, they stand in the dark, rubbing their hands together as if making fire, tendrils of white smoke puffing out of their mouths and nostrils like a train. Then they board outdated yellow or white decades-old buses and go to work. It's a day like any other day. Only colder.

There is a cloudless sky over Immokalee and the air is as crisp as it is quiet. The thousands of heads of well-nourished cattle, the endless rows of produce, and the citrus smell coming from the Duda Juice Concentrate Plant follow me for miles along State Road 27, all the way to Immokalee. All of them give the town a deceiving air of opulence. Immokalee looks almost beautiful.

The door of trailer 42 is open. After knocking at windows and walls all around the trailer, I let myself into the trailer. I call Paulina's name out. No answer. I call her name again. I hear an annoyed moan.

"*Aqui, aqui. Que pasa?* Here, here, what's going on?" I find Paulina in a dark room at the end of the corridor. The windows are covered with pieces of plywood, blocking the light. She is buried somewhere under the sheets.

"Paulina, it's me. Are you OK?"

She emerges from under the covers in slow motion. First comes a matted pony tail, followed by a dirty scrunchy, followed by a frowning forehead, and, finally, Paulina's half-shut eyes.

She tells me that a pinched nerve in the back of her head gives her paralyzing migraines. She invites me to run my fingers across her scalp; four fleshy protuberances claim different spots on her skull. The doctor told her that she needs an operation. No guarantees, though. She'll explain some other day. Not today. She can barely talk. The medicated narcotics make her sleepy. Sorry. I'll have to come back tomorrow.

The following day Paulina is radiant. She is cooking *mole, tamales, gorditas,* and *flautas.* She'll sell them to the farmworkers coming back from the fields in the afternoon. She stops whistling to tell me that she doesn't do agricultural work at the moment.

"My back is all fucked up," she says.

"How much money will you make today?" I ask Paulina while she chops tomatoes.

"Thirty, maybe thirty-five pesos. Good money, don't you think?" she says, using the same linguistic quirk as many other immigrants do: they say pesos but mean dollars.

As she walks back and forth between the kitchen counter and her boiling pots on the stove, she continues her story where we left last time.

A year of hard work in the Immokalee fields had passed when Paulina left her baby girl with a friend and went back to Oaxaca, this time to bury her mother who had died in her sleep. After three weeks in Oaxaca, Paulina was ready to come back to the USA. The river was not an option that Paulina was willing to consider. The sound of the words Piedras Negras alone brought back bad memories: water, death, and that *cabrón chingalamala.* No, this time, Paulina would not cross the Rio Bravo; she'd rather try the desert once more. There had been waves of Mexicans making it across the border with Agua Prieta, a crossing point in Sonora. She liked the sound of it all: the vastness of the desert, the short journey to Tucson, then Phoenix; she even liked the name of the place: *Agua Prieta,* Black Water.

"I had to, had to come back to my girl." Paulina scratches her head with the handle of a butcher's knife. "Hunger, need, and your *chamaquitos* make you do crazy things."

For a few seconds, Paulina disappears behind a curtain of vapor of sautéed onions and shredded pork meat. I'm a vegetarian but the smell makes me reconsider my eating habits.

"Black *Mole,* Oaxacan style, with pork. I hope people like it," Paulina says when I ask her what she's cooking now. "Do you want to know about Mexican food or about my comings and goings?" Paulina asks, half laughing, half serious. "Because if you want to learn how to cook good Mexican food, you're going to have to make another appointment." She laughs over her boiling pots, and so do I over my notebook.

Paulina contacted a coyote. His name was Charlie, a popular *patero* in Agua Prieta, who at some point held the record for the most successful border crossings in six consecutive months. That was good enough for Paulina. The deal was sealed over the phone and a couple of hours later, Paulina and sixteen *campesinos* from the state of Chiapas gathered at Charlie's house to go over the schedule. Charlie had found a weak spot along the ten-foot-high border fence that goes across Agua Prieta. They wouldn't have to climb. It was an easy crossing, he assured them. No ladders, no blowtorches, no fuss. It would be the easiest crossing of their lives, he said, not a bad deal for *pinche* $600.

At three a.m., they had already crossed the border. Charlie made them trot for most of their journey. "This isn't a vacation, *manitos. Orale, rápido que nos coge la migra,* fast before immigration catches us," he repeated for hours. By 10 a.m., Charlie and his group had arrived at a meeting point near Tucson. It was a dingy parking lot on a narrow street in a town with no visible name. They were in the USA. Everything had gone according to plan. They were safe. From then on, they didn't have to do anything; it was all Charlie's work. Just logistics, make sure that everyone else involved in the smuggling was doing his job on time and for the agreed amount. Nothing to do with Paulina or her companions. From then on, it was strictly the coyote's business.

The *raiteros* were waiting for Charlie's group with two vans. In them, they packed the eighteen passengers and took them to Phoenix, where the money transactions between *pollos* and *pollero* were squared. After three days of closed-doors phone calls, trips to the Western Union offices, and high tempers, everybody seemed happy. Charlie got his $10,200 for the trip, his group was in the USA, and a *raitero* was on his way to Phoenix to collect the human cargo he would take to Immokalee, their final destination.

Tightly packed in the van, like sardines, the seventeen immigrants and the driver left Phoenix at eight p.m. They drove along I-17 North towards Flagstaff without a problem. They merged onto I-40 East, stopping only twice to refuel on their way across New Mexico. The driver was cautious at fueling points, allowing only three of his passengers out of the van to use the bathroom. "More than that makes the *bolillos* around suspicious. On this road, there are lots of nosy parkers, *chismosos echando pupila,*" Paulina explains.

By the time the tinted-glassed van made it to Amarillo, Texas, the group was showing signs of dehydration. The air conditioning was broken, there was no ventilation, and the air inside the van became increasingly difficult to breathe. The driver forbade them to roll the windows down but before the sunrise, he stopped at a gas station on the outskirts of Amarillo to get bottles of water.

"He came back in a foul mood and sat in the van throwing bottles of water at us over his shoulder." Paulina mimics the motion of his arm. In the process, she throws a whole tomato over her own shoulder. As she bends down to pick it up, a loud fart escapes her body. She can't stop laughing. She bends forward, knife in hand, then backwards. "I feel lighter now," she says, slapping the kitchen counter with her free hand.

"Anyway," she says. "Two immigration patrol cars boxed in the van and in seconds we were marching, hands behind our heads."

Paulina, the driver, and the other men from Chiapas spent all day and all night in a Texan jail. She doesn't know where. It didn't matter. She had wasted $600 and four days of her life. It was four a.m. when the group woke up to a loud bang on the bars of their jail cell. An immigration agent, baton in hand, instructed them to walk out of the cell in straight line. "*Vamos a la casa,* we're going home," he said with American accent. Home, this time around, was a Mexican town a few yards away from the Texan border.

"They put us in a van and dumped us at a place without name. We didn't even know where we were. It was very early in the morning and everything was closed. I went straight to a public phone and called Charlie. I told him what had happened and that he had to cross us again. He said "You know my fees, *Doña.* For another $600 we'll try a different route but I don't risk my life for free. Put that *pendejo* on the phone. I want him to tell me what happened."

"The driver?" I ask.

"*Sí,* but the driver was still in jail. They let us all go, but they kept the poor *pendejo.*"

Charlie agreed to smuggle them once more, but his flat fee was non-negotiable: $600 each. The group of seventeen Mexicans responded to the news with tears and pleas and threats and more tears. They called relatives and friends over the phone. *More money? What? Six hundred bucks? Are you crazy? We don't have anything left to sell. You think I'm a bank? You still owe me the other trip! You'll never pay me back, pendejo! Orale, don't worry, that's a chingo of money, we need some time, I know Charlie, Charlie is good, I'll talk to your other brothers, your mother, your cousin, your father....*

It took the group three days to get the money. Charlie made them swear on their mothers and daughters that they wouldn't screw him over with the money. "I'll bring your ass back to the border and you won't know on which side of the earth I've dropped you," Charlie threatened.

They left Agua Prieta after the sunset, crossed the same weak spot on the ten-foot-high border fence, walked for seven hours, maybe eight, and prayed all the prayers they knew in their dialects of *Tzeltal* and Spanish. At one point, immigration passed right by them. They ran to the bushes and hid, "like frightened mice," Paulina says. They arrived at the parking lot in Arizona, weary and weak after a week of sleepless nights, hours of walking in the dark, running away, and breathing air," thick like a brick," she tells me. Paulina was the first one in the group to spot the parking lot. She went down on her knees and sent a heart-to-heart message to her little girl: *I'm home, baby, finally I'm going to see you.* But no sooner had Paulina uttered her last word than she saw the first border patrol car, then the second, then the third. Two hours later, the eighteen Mexicans were back on Mexican soil.

"I think they took us to Nogales, but I'm not sure. All you remember is Mexico, the USA, Mexico, the USA. Where in Mexico? Where in the USA? Who cares?"

Paulina hasn't stopped cooking in three hours. In her deranged kitchen of dented pans and grease-stained stove, she looks more like a magician and less like a cook. She throws the butcher knife up in the air like a sushi master and catches it in a split second without looking. Her hair is tied on the back of her neck with a rubber band, but still she keeps tugging strands of loose hair behind her ears. She moves back and forth between the counter and the stove with a fleeting dance of waist contortions: her left leg grounded between the two places and her right leg swinging her body back and forth, counter, stove, stove, counter. She is lively. When she is not talking, she is humming; when she is not humming, she is whistling, and if she is not whistling, she is singing in a murmur a song in *Nahuatl* that she learned when she was a little girl, a lifetime ago.

"We went back to Charlie's house to rest, and the very same night we crossed. This time we crossed for real. It was December; I know that because it was Merry Christmas here and Merry Christmas there, all the way from the *mero* border to Immokalee. When I got here, there was good news and bad news waiting for me. Like I hadn't had enough already!"

The good news was that her little girl was alive, healthy, and desperate to see her mama. The other piece of good news, which Paulina had suspected but didn't have the energy to dwell on, was that she was pregnant again. The bad news was that one of her brothers had died in his sleep.

"Like your mother?"

"*Sí*, it runs in the family," she says.

Paulina turns the stove off and starts packing the food in plastic bags. I don't want to be intrusive, but I want to know about the father of the baby she was expecting when she arrived in Immokalee. I take some more notes while Paulina forms small mounds of packed food on a plastic table.

"Well? Don't you want to know?" she asks. "I met him here in Immokalee before my mother died. We eyed each other and fooled around, but I didn't let him in my bed. He said that he wasn't in a hurry. He'd wait until I was ready. Ready?" Paulina lowers her voice and tiptoes across the room to sit next to me.

There is secrecy and mischief in her broad face. Then a smirk and a wink.

"The twenty-first of March I got one of those fevers. You understand me? A *re-chinga* fever."

"Were you sick?"

"No, not sick. I had the fever. A woman's fever. One of those fevers that makes you want to *chingar medio Mexico*, fuck half of Mexico. So I called him and we slept together."

Paulina sighs and lets out a loud *hmm, hmm, hmm* laden with memories of pure ecstasy.

"Do you want to see his picture?" We laugh at crude bedroom jokes while she looks for his picture. Out of a Formica closet without doors and a broken mirror, Paulina pulls a plastic bag with pictures. "That's him after I gave birth to his baby," she says pointing at a handsome thoroughbred Mexican man leaning back on a rocking chair. He is shirtless, hands interlocked behind his head, with messy black hair and roguish brown eyes. His broad chest tops a tight abdomen full of solid bulges; a thin thread of black hair runs down his torso and under a sparkly belt buckle engraved with the image of the Guadalupe Virgin. He smiles at the camera. I see his white teeth and his fleshy lips despite a thick black mustache that extends beyond the corners of his beautiful mouth.

"He's very handsome," I comment. Paulina explodes in a mocking fit of laughter that sounds like firecrackers.

"That was him when I met him. This is him now," she says, handing me another picture.

A Pancho Villa look-alike man stands by a Bronco car. He's heavy, and an unkempt mustache covers his whole mouth. He is not smiling at the camera. He looks tough under the shade of his large white hat. His arms are crossed over his chest, macho style, as if showing off the rings he has on every finger except his thumbs. His enormous white cowboy boots make him look shorter, and his swollen cheeks add ten years to his face. He's wearing a red and white shirt that looks too small for his protruding belly. There is nothing roguish about him. I'm looking at the picture of an old fat man.

"What happened? He looks very different here."

"This happened," Paulina says, pointing at the food. "There is nothing to do here other than work and eat tortillas. We're happy? We eat tortillas. We're sad? We eat tortillas. Breakfast, lunch and dinner? More tortillas. If it weren't for these *chinga* tortillas we wouldn't have anything to eat. Have you seen the prices of food? *Eeholai,* thank God for tortillas."

It's not just the tortilla diet that sustains farmworkers that ages them; it's the sun, the sometimes more than 100 degrees they work under during the summer, the cold of the freezing mornings during the winter, the pesticides they inhale in the fields, the squalor of their living quarters, the abandonment and anonymity their immigration status condemns them to. It's the sorrow of not being able to go back to their land to bury their dead, the low glass ceiling that their children bang their heads against after high school, the language barrier, the complexity of a system they can't fathom. It's the inexplicable miscarriages, the long lines at charity organizations, the hurricanes that every year destroy what little they have, the accumulation of frustrations that explode at home in kicks and punches; it's the violence and its inherent secrecy, it's the secrecy and its innate impunity, it's the impunity and its inescapable hopelessness.

"Are you living with Pancho Villa here?" I ask Paulina. She bursts out laughing at the sound of the words Pancho Villa.

"I'm going to tell him that *la doña* called him Pancho Villa." Paulina stops laughing. "Men are nothing but trouble. Even this one." Paulina taps the picture. "All men are *perros chingalamalas*. But when I get the fever? That's different. Then I call him and he makes me happy. But as soon as we're done, I show him the door so he doesn't think I'm his wife or something."

"And is he OK with that?"

"No, but that has nothing to do with me. I say, living with a man? *ni a bala,* never. If he likes it, fine. And if doesn't, tough titty. It's his loss. Immokalee is full of single men."

"Why don't you want to live with him? Doesn't he treat you right?"

"Like a princess. On weekends he takes me and my kids to the *taqueria* and sometimes to McDonald's to eat hamburgers. But that's it. I don't want to end up like my sister."

"What's wrong with Simona?"

"Didn't she tell you?"

"No, what?"

"In that case, I won't tell you either. I don't talk about people behind their backs. But I'll tell you this, her husband *es un hijo de la chingada,* a son of a *chingada. Un re-que-te-cabrón.*"

"Where is she now?"

"Working in the fields, *pizcando* tomatoes, oranges, anything. She is still paying the money she borrowed from everyone to pay her coyote."

"How much did she pay?"

"*Un chingo* of money. She had to fly from Mexico City to Miami. She has a little boy. Haven't you seen him? He's deaf and mute and too small to walk the desert or swim across the river. No coyote would bring a three-year-old boy across. Anyway, what did you ask me? Oh yes, the price. She paid $2,500 for her ticket and $1,800 for the boy's."

"How did she do that? Did she have a passport?" I ask, confused.

"*Pos no.* That's why it's so expensive. Her coyote gave her fake American passports with their pictures and their names on them. They know how to do it. Lots of gringos sell their passports. That's their business. Simona showed the passports at the airport in Mexico, got on the plane, landed in Miami, and as soon as she got their passports checked in immigration, another coyote took the passports away. See? To re-sell them. That's how it works."

"Do you think that she'd talk to me, like you did?"

"I don't think so. She's always in a rotten mood, not like me. She doesn't say much to anyone and anyway, she's sick. Didn't you see how skinny she is? All bones."

"Maybe she needs more of your tortillas," I say casually.

"That's all she eats. I think it's the tortilla diet that's killing her," Paulina says as she walks towards the door with her bag of exquisite-smelling cargo. "You need to go, *Doña*. I have to make some money to pay the *beeless,* the bills." She locks the trailer behind us and starts walking away from me without looking back.

"Good bye, Paulina. Thank you for sharing your..." she doesn't let me finish. She waves her free arm in the air and tells me she's not fond of goodbyes and *chingadas.*

She wears a fleece jacket two sizes too big for her and a pair of home-altered jeans with hand-sewn hems. That and a plastic bag full of Mexican food that, I'm sure, feels warm and comforting on her back. She stops at the end of the narrow street that divides the trailer park into two and turns around. I expect a *goodbye*, but instead she twists her open hand in the air and says: *Orale manita!* See ya, sis! Then she turns right and disappears.

Letter to My Mother

Mama,

Last week when I called you to wish you a happy Mother's Day, you asked me about my ongoing project with undocumented women and wanted to know why I'm so hell-bent on finding Esperanza. I don't know, mama. I guess a part of me still is fourteen years old and fervently believes in change, social justice and the redeemable power of the written word. That part of me wants to make a difference, give voice to two, three, four women whose plight would otherwise go unheeded. I want to make the powers that be uncomfortable enough with my narrative to prompt a revaluation of immigration laws. Foolish, I know. But I'm your daughter, I inherited your stubbornness and your faith in that religion women become when they gang up against the world.

Mama, I also think that I want to find Esperanza because she reminds me of you. I see you migrating from place to place with four, five, six children in tow. Making it across the Andes, wading the waters of the Magdalena River, trudging from corner to corner of the streets of Armenia, Fresno, Bogotá, the whole of Colombia all the way beyond the Ecuadorian border which you once crossed with nothing but a splinter of hope and a suitcase of fortitude. You might say that it's not the same. That you were not undocumented, that your struggle didn't involve being chased by immigration officers, that you never had to eat desert snakes or moisten our chapped lips with your own saliva, or dive into the rapid-churned waters of the Rio Bravo. But you crossed state and country borders for us, just like Esperanza did for her children. That is why I'm so hell-bent on finding a woman who, as you put it, I don't even know and who might not want to awaken the past.

The thing is, mama, I think I know her. Sometimes I fall asleep imagining parts of her. She'll have your dexterous, venous hands. Hands that fix, feed, straighten, caress and spank all with the same conviction. She'll have eyes that can see right through cement. Unblinkingly scrutinizing eyes a little slanted towards the ears, slowly gliding in tandem with her cheeks. Eyes that, just like yours, tear up only at night while the world slumbers. The other night, I fell asleep thinking that she was curvy, delicate, and sensuous, with diminutive waist, generous breasts, round hips and luscious hair. She looked at an imaginary camera and smiled a coy smirk full of small, even teeth. Then she blew a kiss with her fleshy lips and that's when I realized that I was thinking of Salma Hayek. She's a Mexican actress, mama. Do you know her? Ask my sisters to rent *Frida* and promise me not to fall asleep like you always do during movies.

Mama, Esperanza has children, you have yours, I have mine. See the bond? We are mothers, therefore sisters. We belong to a tribe of women warriors. We are beasty creatures with feral habits. We have long claws that rip the flesh of our predators and fiery beaks that peck and gouge. We look motherly and defenseless as we breastfeed our babies but at the smallest hint of danger, a sudden change in the direction of the winds or a tide two inches too far ashore and the machetes fly out of the sheaths. We shriek with voices dark like tinted glass and whistles that burn the ears like cigarettes. We're mothers. We're dangerous.

A few years back when I was living in Alaska you had a day of absolute lucidity. Remember? I took you to Mirror Lake and you, my daughter and I had a little picnic by its pristine waters. You took a day off from Alzheimer's and we told each other jokes, gossiped about my sisters, and talked about Dad, whom neither of us had seen in over ten years. Then I asked you about the time you were pregnant with me. And you told me without hesitation that I had not been planned; that I, your sixth child, had not been wanted: a revelation that I could not reconcile with a life filled with nothing but your fierce devotion and relentless love for me. And I wonder now if Esperanza felt the same way about the baby she lost while trekking the desert. Maybe she did not want to bring another baby into her world of poverty and neglect. But she gave birth to her and loved her all the same, maybe even a little more than she loved her older children just like you always told me you loved me more than you loved my siblings. That's how it works, right, mama? We have our doubts while we carry them in our internal marsupial pouch, but when we hold them in our arms the doubts grow wings and fly fast and furious out of our lives.

When I was in high school you reprimanded me for bringing home a poster of Parvati, the Hindu goddess. There was only one God, you said, He was Catholic, had a son named *Jesús* and a representative on earth called The Pope. Had you not shredded it to pieces, had you listened to me, I would have told you that the poster represented you: a woman with divine attributes, the Goddess of the household, marriage, motherhood and family. What I liked about Parvati was that she was depicted carrying lotus flowers with delicate hands and taking tiny strides with dainty feet when in the presence of her husband, Shiva. But when alone, she had two, four, sometimes six arms, omnipresent and ever-reaching tentacles, and she rode a tiger or a lion bareback. Mama, she is ferocious, her strength and powers have no limit when alone. Like you. You are the embodiment of Parvati and so is Esperanza.

Does this answer your question about being hell-bent on finding an undocumented woman I have never seen? Maybe not, but it will have to do until I find her. And when the day arrives, I'll tell her about you, and about my sisters, my aunts, my girlfriends, me. I'll tell her all about the women who've crossed my path. I'll tell her about Parvati and maybe, if she allows me, I'll give her a poster of the goddess.

Laura

On my way to Wimauma, a small agricultural community in Central Florida, I drive through Sun City, a community of middle-class retirees located less than ten miles away from Wimauma. These two towns have little to nothing in common; their ethnic makeup tells a tale of its own. Sun City is ninety-eight percent white; Wimauma, on the other hand, is seventy-three percent Hispanic. Everything else is history. The median income for a family in Sun City is $47,500 while the per capita income for Wimauma is $8,500, putting more than half of its population below the poverty line.

How could two neighboring towns a mere fifteen-minute drive from each other be so different? What has kept the wealth of American retirees from advancing into Wimauma or the Hispanic workers from flooding the labor market in Sun City?

"Skin color," Javier says. He is young, short, lean, dark and speaks in colorful spanglish.

"You can *watchearlos* from your *trocka* and judge for yourself. Americans play *golfo* over there in Sun City. They get pink under the sun and they like it. They think pink is the same as tan. But you drive a few minutes east and you find us Mexicans *pizcando* in the *feel,* the field. We get all dark even under big-ass hats."

Javier works as operations manager at a farmworker ministry in Wimauma, one of the many centers across Florida that provide a wide range of services to the Hispanic community. He tells me that he could have been a *roofero,* a roofer, after he left the fields. Instead he went to a community college and earned a degree in Human Services.

"I couldn't bear the thought of being up on roofs day in and day out looking for *leakeos.* I wanted to help my people, immigrants like me, you know?"

He is an American citizen, but Javier is, above all, a Mexican man. It's as though the border with the USA runs right through the middle of his heart, bisecting him into two. That's probably why Javier chose to keep an intimate contact with the realities of the Mexico he loves and misses through the people he helps every day to find affordable housing.

I'm here to inquire about Esperanza. Maybe she came to this place looking for help—maybe looking for a temporary shelter, maybe for a permanent dwelling, nothing fancy, the simplest would have done. I wonder if she got a small off-white trailer that she later painted in shades of terracotta, blue and mustard. I wonder if on weekends she picked wild flowers and put them in plastic vases by the window, then watched them wilt during the week.

"Do you remember ever talking to a woman named Esperanza Vasquez?" I ask Javier.

His dark mouth bends downwards. He squints a little; his eyes take a lazy dive into a painting on the wall. "She Mexican?" I nod. "She from around here?" he asks.

"She is Mexican but I don't know if she is from around here. I'm looking for her. She lost a baby during the crossing. Have you heard anything like that?"

"You hear stuff like that very often, but you *forgetas* the names. You should talk to my *waifa*. She works in the *feels*, maybe she knows something."

He agrees to call his wife and arrange a meeting so that I can interview her. He dials the number of her *celfon* and presses the speaker button on. The telephone rings a few times; then I hear his own voice at the other end. *I can't come to the phone right now. Leave a message after the bip and te hablo pa'tras as soon as I can.*

"The *waifa* doesn't like the sound of her voice," he explains.

That same evening I met Laura, Javier's wife. She's tall and nowhere near as lean as Javier. Her arms are tanned and muscular, her face patchy after years under the sun, her hair dull, her frame burly. She wears tight blue jeans, a Coca Cola t-shirt, and a pair of imitation Nike shoes. Inside her impeccable house, she moves a lot—cleaning, dusting, moving this and that from here to there—talks fast, and changes topics at a racing pace. I try and instantly fail to keep up with her. I feel sluggish and dry in her vibrant presence.

It's eight p.m. She invites me to sit in the porch. A warm October breeze passes through, stroking our faces on its way west. I sit on a rocking chair. Laura fiddles around with flowers, toys, her pony tail, the broom, and everything else she deems in need of her attention while she talks. No, she doesn't know Esperanza Vasquez. And no, she knows nothing about a woman losing a baby crossing *el borde*.

Finally, Laura sits in a rocking chair next to mine.

"Nobody likes to talk about the past. Most of the women out in the *feels* have crossed *el borde* on foot, if they walked the desert, or on their bellies, if they swam the river; but nobody, *nobody* talks about the crossing itself." Laura places both hands on her thighs and moves her body forward. "Once you're here, there is no time to look back or feel sorry for yourself. You get to work, send your *chamacos* to school, take care of your man, make money, and that's it. You don't go around moping."

Sometimes I wonder if I'm the only one "moping." I wonder if Esperanza has already locked her loss in a black box and thrown away the key. I wonder if by the time I find her, if I ever do, she'll refuse to exhume the memories of her baby buried now under layers of sand, time, and tears.

I press the rec button of my tape recorder but Laura says no. She doesn't like to leave her voice behind. "My voice is mine. I carry it with me. Didn't Javier warn you?" I agree to take notes but ask her to be gentle with my fingers and to be patient as I suspect it'll be hard to keep up with her.

Laura and Javier are American citizens from Brownsville, Texas. They built their own house on an acre of green land. They have two cars, a purebred Chihuahua, and three children who say good evening, please, and thank you in unaccented English. I ask Laura why she works in the fields when she could be doing anything else.

"Who? Me?" she asks, surprised. "I never went to school. Look at my hands," she says, stretching her calloused hands palms-up in the air. "I helped Javier build this house with these very hands. How else do you think poor Mexicans reach the American dream? Working our asses off, that's how."

She describes herself as a dark, poor, illiterate Mexican. For women like herself, she says, American citizens or not, there is nothing to do but work hard. Besides, Christmas is coming up and having three American kids in Florida is not the same as having three Mexican kids in Tamaulipas. This Christmas, Javier and Laura need to be able to come up with the regular essentials for their children: new clothes, shoes, white socks and handkerchiefs for the boys, and have I noticed that American men don't use hankies? Additionally, the boys want a computer with Internet access and an X-box, or at least a Play Station II because apparently everybody else in their classrooms has one or all of them. A computerless family that possesses no video games is an oddity by today's American standards. So far, they have stood odd and proud, but Laura is determined to drop the "odd" and stick with the "proud" before the end of the year. And on top of that, Laura goes on, presents aside, December is a month like any other, with mortgage payments, utility bills, car installments, and trips to the grocery store.

How do they do it? How can they afford three children, two cars, a house and a purebred Chihuahua? The secret lies in a combination of two traits, one inherited from their Mexican ancestors and one acquired from the modern American culture: hard work and credit. Like millions of Americans, Laura and Javier don't own what they have. They owe it all: the house, the cars, a living room set paid eighteen months interest-free, good-as-cash style, and an orthodontic treatment—not covered by his health insurance—for one of their boys.

"Right now, we're planting strawberries. It doesn't pay well, which is good because it forces you to be resourceful and it keeps you on your toes," Laura says. "You know what I mean?" she asks. I shake my head "no."

"You have to, what's the word? Diversify, I think. You plant strawberries, then you go and pick some tomatoes and then go to the packing house and put some extra hours there, then we're talking big money, see how it works?"

"What kind of big money are we talking about?" I ask.

She scratches her neck, slaps a mosquito on her forearm, and says, "Work fifteen hours a day and you get up to eighty dollars. Big money, *si o no?*"

I don't know why but right at this moment I feel the need to change my research strategy. I want to be out with the farmworkers. I want to shadow Laura, stop taking notes, get my hands dirty and experience in my own skin what it's like to work fifteen hours a day for eighty dollars.

"Can I go to the field with you?" I ask, but she looks at me as if I have said something ridiculous.

"You? In the *field?*" Laura shakes her head. "*Heeeeeeh,* that's for machos. Look at you. You're so thiiiin. You need quick feet, fast hands," Laura says, snapping her fingers. I promise not to be in her way. I tell her that I'll be her student in the field, if she agrees to be my teacher.

"Let me tell you, it's hard work, it's filthy, and I start early," Laura says, in another attempt to discourage me.

"I'm an early bird, Laura. And so you know, I'm stronger than I look."

"If you're not here by five a.m., I'll leave without you." Laura taps her scratched watch. "Bring a long-sleeved shirt, rubber gloves, a hat so you don't cook, a comfy pair of trousers, and old shoes because they'll be a mess by the time you finish. If you finish at all," she says patting my knee with an open hand. "You are cuckoo in the head," she adds.

I'm pumped up and I feel a little cocky about this. I live in Central Florida. I've seen the fields. I've watched people plow, plant, harvest. It doesn't look that difficult. I work out every day at the gym. I have a special relationship with the treadmill and never miss my spinning classes. I'm fit. I figure the experience will be all about finding ways to adjust the body to get it used to certain positions. When in pain, our bodies naturally shift weight, alternate postures, control breathing. Besides, the body can use extra help from the mind, I think. A combination of physical strength and meditation will get me through the experience.

It's 4:45 a.m. Laura has already made coffee for both of us and breakfast for Javier. She has already fixed lunches for her children and taken everybody's clothes out of the dryer. She opens the door for me but doesn't greet me; instead, she grabs me by my hoodie and pulls me into the kitchen. She is methodic, fast, robotic even as she washes dishes and sweeps bread crumbs off the kitchen counter. Laura does all of this while pressing the phone between her right shoulder and ear. When she is done with the bread crumbs, she grabs a broom and sweeps the kitchen floor. I can tell that she is talking to a few crew leaders in the area. She stops doing chores only to write down the addresses of the strawberry fields where labor is needed today. She retrieves mental maps of the area and asks the crew leaders for landmarks: close to the church, behind the 7-Eleven, around the corner from *la taqueria*, off Highway 60, parallel to County Line Road, next to this or that farm. Laura chooses to go to work for the crew leader whose farm is closer, to save on gas, she says, and while she ushers me out of the house, she grabs the broom and sweeps the floor with furious, hurried lashes. We leave her house floating in an invisible goblet of aromas: toothpaste, fresh coffee, peanut butter sandwiches, home.

"*El bolillo* is shorthanded this morning. I'm calling Maria and Don Pedro, and Perla," Laura tells me while she cleans the passenger's seat of her van for me. Her van is the antithesis of her pristine house. The back seats are a medley of muddy shoes, toys, dented Pepsi cans, coins, school books, and empty lunch pails. She starts the van and reverses out of her driveway without looking back. I'm still sluggish from my early start. Laura, on the other hand, seems unstoppable. She drinks her coffee from a chipped Starbucks mug and talks on her *celfon* simultaneously. At one point, I see her holding the coffee mug with one hand and dialing a number with the other. She steers with her knees.

Twenty minutes later, before the sun rises, we arrive at the strawberry field. In the crepuscular predawn light, we look like we are part of someone's dream. We are nebulous ghosts moving in that fluid middle space between a slumbering Florida and a fully awake community of immigrant workers. Thirty acres of fertile ground give us a foggy welcome. The wind pounds on the black plastic that covers line after line of trapezoidal plant beds, making a shh, shh, shh noise that reverberates in the atmosphere like distant cymbals. The air is fresh, the clouds thick and gray. I'm full of energy.

I look at the field and the other day laborers as they arrive. Some know each other and exchange hurried *"buenas"* while they put on the rubber gloves. There are people of all ages; some look as old as late sixties, like Don Pedro, while others seem to be still in their teens, their faces bursting with pimples and teeth that have never seen an orthodontist.

At the end of the field is a truck loaded with white cardboard boxes, and at the opposite end, too far away for anyone to walk to it, is a green portable toilet. As more workers arrive, the field explodes in spontaneous outbursts of life. Everybody seems to know where to go and what to do. The laborers assume positions and execute tasks too fast for me to follow. I'm looking over the rows for Laura when I hear the voice of the crew leader shouting at me:

"Vas a trabajar o que? Are you working or what?" I say *"Si"* and almost miss a twenty-five-pound carton box he flings at me from the back of his truck. It's a confusing piñata of boxes raining out of his hands and into the hands of all of us farmworkers. I spot Laura at the end of a row and run towards her with my box. Time is of the essence here, she tells me without words, as she rips the box open. Inside it is a wet mass of strawberry plants bundled with rubber bands in groups of twenty-five. The plants are small, their roots muddy and tangled up. We have to remove the rubber bands, separate one plant from the other, and sow them individually in the evenly-spaced holes perforated along the rows of beds. These trapezes are about a half-mile long by one foot tall and are wrapped with thick plastic sheeting that keeps moisture and fertilizers in place.

I look at the others to see how it's done. I still believe there is nothing to it. If the plant is either too big or too small, I throw it to one side. If the plant is a medium size, I plant it in each pre-cut hole on the plastic sheet. We bend at the waist over the row. Laura recites a string of instructions as we start to move to the left, down the row. Leave the red bottom part of the stems out. Quick. Make sure you bury only the roots. Fast. Push them into the hole with two fingers. *Rápido.* Cover the roots with a bit of soil. *Andale.* I'm bent over the plastic, legs stretched out, feet a bit apart. Piece of cake, I think as I plant my first two, three, then four strawberry plants. I feel an enormous sense of accomplishment.

Laura and I are working on opposite sides of the same row. We face each other only for a few minutes. The holes on her side fill with green, cold strawberry plants at the speed of light. For one second, I see the empty hole and in the blink of an eye, the hole disappears under Laura's expert hands. The space between my row and the row behind me is not big enough for my feet to lay flat on the ground. I shift them around, pointing outward, then inward, then heels up against the row behind. I want to ask Laura what the best position to do this is, but she is moving away from me at a furious pace. She bends at the waist, moving so fast from hole to hole that all I can think of is cartoon characters and how she moves just like them: from one place to another without apparently being anywhere in between.

Out of all the posture variations I try as I move left trying to catch up with Laura, bending at the waist is probably the most unnatural position to work. I improvise some poses that make other workers smile with pity. After a variety of useless acrobatics I realize that stooping is the only way to do it. Since there is no room to stand up with my feet flat on the ground separating the rows, let alone to crawl on my shins, neither kneeling nor squatting is an option. By the time I'm done with my twentieth plant, the muscles of my lower back bunch up in a large knot. I can feel it with my gloved hand like a speed bump.

I look around. It is a mad race. And nobody is tired yet. Men and women, their heads down at knee height, move up and down the rows of their choice. The sooner they finish with a box of plants, the sooner they get the next one, and the next one, and the next one, until they finish their rows. At the end, there will be a friendly race for the last two left in the field.

I play mental games to keep my mind off the lumbar pain. I try to sing *Amazing Grace* under my breath, but I can't remember the lyrics. I try something in Spanish, but the words of my song get muddled with a Mexican *ranchera* blaring out of a radio transistor strapped to Don Pedro's belt. The pain in my back increases with each passing hour. I aim for what psychologists call "flow state," a Zen-like nirvana during which sense organs transmit signals directly to the muscles, bypassing the cerebral cortex, and I fail miserably. Instead, pain sets in.

"Now what?" I ask Laura after I finish my first box. Although I've been looking forward for the moment to straighten my back, something in the space between my kidneys, like a rusted short spring, forces me back into a hunch. Laura laughs and shakes her head.

"Run to the truck with the empty box to get paid and get another one. *Andale niña, métele ganas!*"

I do as I'm told. The crew leader takes my empty box, hands me a blue chip, and gives me another twenty-five-pound box of plants. By the time I come back to Laura, she is already halfway through a new row.

"The crew leader gave me this," I say to Laura showing her the blue chip. "When do we get paid?"

"At the end of the day you give him back the tokens and he writes the number on a paper next to your name," she says, her eyes on the ground. From a distance, I'm sure she looks demented, as if she was talking to the earth.

"On Fridays you get your cash. It's payday, baby. Fridays are happy days. Isn't it true, *muchachos?*" Laura asks looking around over her shoulders. A murmur of *si, si,* rises in the air.

Farmworkers get paid by the box, each token representing a box of twenty-five pounds of plants. Or at least that's what the crew leader says. As far as I'm concerned, he could say thirty pounds, or thirty-five or fifteen. I wouldn't know the difference.

"But how much is each token? And how do you know that all boxes weigh the same?" I ask Laura.

"Don't know and don't know," Laura says, her eyes moving from hole to hole. I prod.

"You don't know how much you get paid?" I try to ask and move at the same time but I can't multitask right now. I'm in agonizing pain, confused by the finances of the business and falling behind.

"No. I told you. You wait until Friday."

"But how do you know that what you get paid on Friday is fair?"

"If you work hard and the pay is good, that's fair, right?" Laura is emphatic. Her statement is not an invitation to a debate. It's a simple mathematical operation, not a dissertation on fairness or social justice.

I ask the three women planting the row behind me. Nobody knows what the going rate is. I might as well be asking about the price of crude oil. Laura says that I ask the funniest questions. The other women smile, amused.

"If you work like a mule and your pay is fat, then you go home happy," Don Pedro says. I look at him over my left shoulder. He's two rows back, bent over the field, his thick mustache glistening with sweat. That's all I see, that and his enormous hands going in and out of the earth.

"If you're sick and you can't work as hard as everybody else, you find out on Friday because you receive little money," Don Pedro says, already ten feet away from where he was a few seconds ago.

Our notions of fairness are worlds apart. Don Pedro is illiterate and innumerate. He signs with a cross and keeps track of his tokens with sticks that he marks with a pen on his fingers: The thumb is Monday, the index is Tuesday, three sticks on his pinky because he was sick on Friday, five sticks on his middle finger because on Wednesday he worked *like a mule.*

The farmworkers don't stretch, don't talk much, don't ask for breaks, don't use the toilet, don't eat, don't drink. Nobody tells them that they can't do any of these things, but hunger and need speak louder than the crew leaders. If they stop, somebody else will finish the row for them, somebody else will make the extra buck or two they need to buy tortillas and beans, or a pound of Maseca flour, their staple.

By midmorning, I'm working my way through the third box. The pain is excruciating. My calves cramp from the prolonged outstretch standing position, the back of my neck twitches as if rising in protest, and my toenails start to feel the effects of being pushed forward on a slanted terrain. I can't straighten my back, nor can I hunch or crouch; no position gives me relief. A part of me wants to quit. I want to shout to Laura that it has been a great experience but I'm not cut for it. But another part of me wants to keep up with old Don Pedro and curvy Laura; this part of me envies their strength, their dexterity, their grace, even, and I decide to plod on although I'm on the verge of tears.

We've been working for a few hours and it's beginning to rain. Nobody stops working. Neither do I. The drizzle turns into a shower and the shower into heavy rain. It rains hard on our necks and backs. Rivulets of water run down our faces, making it difficult to see. Our trousers get heavy, and our shoes squirt water with each step we take. Laura asks me to stop. She says that if I was curious, I've probably already seen enough. I could rest in her van and wait for her, if I want to, she says. I say "no." I'm determined to stay.

We finish the thirty acres in less than six hours. Our clothes are still damp from the rain. I'm the only one shivering. The field has lost its black and plastic makeup. Tiny green plants flutter their leaves in all directions, filling the field with brand-new life. Everybody starts a slow march towards the truck where the crew leader counts the tokens and writes the number next to their names.

There are two coolers open on the bed of the crew leader's truck, one with sodas and one with beers. A young man, who is clearly not old enough to drink, takes two beers, tucks them in the back pockets of his baggy jeans and walks away with another two, one in each hand. Behind him follow his two pimple-faced buddies. They do the same. These beers are lagniappe, a little perk to keep good workers coming back for more of the same.

It is a different world out here in the fields. A world with no child labor rules, no compulsory schooling for minors, no smoking or drinking age limit. The teenagers here are not where our society dictates they should be: playing sports, singing in choirs, taking tests, rehearsing how to be grown-ups. Instead they're here being men. This is no rehearsal.

I hand my six tokens to Laura. She puts them together with hers and gives them to the crew leader. After he records the transaction, Laura says a quiet *has-*

ta mañana. I urge her to ask him how much we're getting paid, but she refuses.

"Crew leaders don't like *preguntones,* people who ask too many questions," she says, and starts walking to her van.

"If I ask too many questions the next time I come they say 'No *doña*, gracias, I don't need more people today,' and I have to go home empty-handed and *pos no se puede!* It can't be!" Laura says, as she slides open the door of her van. I don't want to upset her, but I can't follow her either. I need to know how much our effort was worth. This is not my livelihood, I think. I'm not planning on coming back and if I do and I'm sent home empty-handed as Laura says, there is always another field in another farm in another county.

I ask the crew leader, a young Chicano man with brusque manners, how many plants were in each box.

"Don't know," he mumbles through a wad of chewing tobacco.

"Can you find out?" I ask. The other farmworkers distance themselves from me as if making a *We don't know her* statement.

The young man spits a black gob that dies a mere inch away from the tip of my muddy shoes, which I imagine was the intended destination of the spit. He's annoyed. He's not used to being questioned. He flips receipts without looking and repeats that he doesn't know. I tell him, I'm not in a hurry. I can wait until he finds out. The farmworkers disperse quickly; some of them look at me from their cars. And so does Laura, who is now cleaning her windshield with a damp cloth. She looks as vigorous as she was at 4:45 a.m.

Six hundred and twenty-five, the young man says as if enlightened by a sudden epiphany. It's obvious that he knew the number all along. Six hundred and twenty-five ? I ask, or rather repeat. "If that's what you heard, that's what I said," the crew leader mumbles. So by the end of the morning I have planted 3,750 plants, a pitiful amount by all standards; that is 750 plants per hour, or twelve per minute, one every five seconds. But still, I don't know how much money we're getting paid. I take a chance again.

"How much are you paying us today?"

"Twelve for a thousand" the crew leader says and starts locking the bed of his truck. I'm still in the dark. I can't translate his fragmented information into cash. I ask him again. He repeats with his most condescending vocalization.

"Twelve-dollars-for-each-thousand-plants," the young Chicano says as he gets behind the wheel.

Most of the people in the field cannot write or read, let alone do mental mathematics. Neither can I at the moment. I try for a few minutes but I'm too exhausted to play with numbers. I'm sufficiently humbled and have by now gained the kind of respect for the farmworkers that can only be acquired by laboring along with them in the field. My legs feel like rubber one minute, like lead the next. I start to walk towards the van, but an invisible pain forces my knees apart and makes me walk like an old ape. I can't help it. I do as I'm told by my body. I take tiny strides; my feet sink and slide sideways in the mud while Laura pads nimbly over the ground around her van. Walking through the fields with Laura is like swimming with a dolphin.

All of the others have already left. They'll be planting again tomorrow and the day after; they'll stoop under the rain or under the sun, someone will bring a radio transistor that'll blast out *border corridos,* and to the beats of strumming Mexican guitars, they'll plant thousands of strawberries without knowing how much their labor is worth.

"Ayayayyy, *mira nada mas,* look at you," Laura says with a mocking grin as I plunge into the passenger's seat—my buttocks, calves, lower back and neck wanting to go different places and into different bodies. Our clothes are dirty beyond salvaging, our faces splashed with mud and soil from the entangled, wet roots, our hair in knots from the rain, the sun and the wind. We look like victims of a mudslide, but underneath the muck lay two different women: a weak, broken one, me, and an unbreakable, vivacious, exuberant beyond words one, Laura.

"How does a Mexican know it's time to eat?" Laura asks. I'm confused. "It's a joke. Don't you like jokes?"

"Aren't you tired?" I ask Laura. I'm drained and in no mood for jokes.

"As tired as you are, *manita.* I've been doing this for twenty years and believe me, it doesn't get any easier. I still go home and have my Ibuprofens before going *a la pizca de tomates.*" Laura says as she reverses the van out of the field, the same way she did it this morning out of her driveway, without looking back.

"I had forgotten about the tomatoes this afternoon," I say, feeling crushed by an invisible weight. I can't even fasten my seat belt, let alone do more of the same in a different field.

"Don't worry. I need to go home anyway to make proper lunch for the children. You can take your car and go home." She stops at the first red traffic light and takes a god look at me.

"What?" I ask.

"You look like you're ready to pass out," Laura says, her tongue sticking out of her mouth, her eyes rolled back, her face tilted to one side lifeless. That's Laura doing me. I force a smile.

"You do this every day? I mean, six hours planting strawberries, then home to cook, later on put some hours picking tomatoes, and then more hours at the packing house? When do you rest?"

Laura takes a long sip from her cold Sprite. "Planting is the easiest job there is," she scoffs, and takes another sip of her green bottle. "We *campesinos* move along with nature. We rest when the soil rests: during the summer. That's when some Mexicans go North to the Carolinas, but me? I don't go anywhere. I have my family here. I don't leave Florida. I work until the ground says no more."

I use the calculator in Laura's *celfon*. She laughs. She thinks it's funny that I'm determined to find out how much we'd have been paid today. The final number appears on the screen: forty-five dollars.

"Now, be honest with me," I ask Laura. "Do you think that all the work we did this morning is worth forty-five dollars?"

"For planting? Yeah, it's not bad. It looks better when you add the tomato picking and the packing. Remember, there is no work in Florida from mid-May to mid-August. I don't get paid during the summer. So, I work, work, work wherever anyone needs a hand."

Laura starts a second round of phone calls as she drives. She is trying to find a shorthanded crew leader at any nearby tomato grove. "The more people they need, the more friends I can bring along. We're like old donkeys. We scratch each other's backs."

"I don't know how you do it," I say with a mixture of affection and respect. Laura doesn't respond. She taps the wheel to the beat of an inaudible song—some happy beat that only she can hear. Possibly the beat of her relentless heart.

"If you want, you can come tomorrow cherry tomato picking. They pay up to two dollars for each waist-high hamper. You rest today and you'll be like new tomorrow. What do you say?"

I want to have the courage to accept her invitation, but I know deep down that I'll need more than a few hours to recuperate. Instead I tell her a pitiful lie.

"Sounds good but I have some interviews lined up for tomorrow. Maybe next week."

"Sure," she says, and I know she can see right through my pathetic line.

"Well, don't you want to know?" Laura asks, rescuing me from the depths of shame.

"What?"

"How does a Mexican know when it's time to eat?" She purses her lips trying not to laugh.

"How?"

"When his asshole stops hurting."

It takes me a while to get the joke, which makes Laura laugh even harder. She bobs her head back and forth, the sunlight caresses her face through the windshield and she laughs with gusto. Her head jerks with each chortle. She looks like she is performing a courtship dance. She tells me two more Mexican jokes and she laughs some more—at my dullness, at herself, at life.

Laura opens the door and motions me in. Her house is spotless. A whiff of lavender-scented disinfectant envelops the house as I sit on a stool at the kitchen counter. Laura is again on the phone, this time with a woman called Juanita. "We need to pick her up," Laura whispers at me covering the mouthpiece of the phone with her hand. "She can't drive. Long story," Laura says a few seconds later.

"Get ready. We'll go to the packing house today," I hear her say while she writes down the directions to Juanita's home.

Laura is set in her ways. We get into her van, and she reverses without looking back or using the mirrors. She takes sips of coffee, calls some other people on the phone, steers with her knees.

"We're not going to the field today?" I ask.

"No, I can't bend over today. Estoy *reglando*, I'm periurding," she says, using another peculiar linguistic quirk common among some Mexican farmworkers of turning any noun into a verb in either English or Spanish. If a woman is on her period, she is periurding; to tie plants in a bunch becomes *bunchiar*, and today we'll be *claseando*, classifying tomatoes according to color.

Laura's van bounces off down a dwindling dirt road, tossing us around. I hit my knee against the glove compartment. Shit. Laura bangs her head against the window. Fuck.

"Did Javier tell you?" she asks, massaging the right side of her head where she just banged it.

"What?"

"How he and his family got here?"

"No."

"Didn't think so. He doesn't like to talk about it. He says that the past is called *past* for a reason."

Laura starts the story with words of caution, "This happened a long time ago," and she wags her index as if summoning me to recall whatever she is about to tell me as history, a decades-old, almost forgotten past.

Javier was fourteen when his father, a shrimp merchant in Brownsville, Texas, decided to follow the steps of other Mexicans who had left for El Norte in search of good fortune. They had gone to a place in Florida called Plant City, where, everybody said, there was work all year round, sunshine, beaches and everything a Mexican could ever dream of. Javier's old man liked the idea. He'd find work at a big shrimp company. His children would work in fields bursting with mouthwatering strawberries. His wife would run the house, cooking, cleaning. She would bring him glasses of cold lemonade to a white hammock he'd hang on the porch of their house, then she would tease him into bed, where they'd make more American children.

He drove his family north to Corpus Christi, then to San Antonio where they took Interstate 10 East bound. That's all the directions the old man had. I-10 would take them straight to beautiful Plant City, he was told. It was a simple plan. In Houston, he stopped and asked a passerby, "Is this Florida already?" No. He had a long way to go. In Louisiana, he asked the attendant at a gas station, "Is this Plant City?" No. He wasn't yet in Florida. He was in New Orleans. He'd never heard of such a place and kept on driving. In Tallahassee, he looked for a Mexican and damned himself for never having learned English. "Is this Plant City?" No, it wasn't, but he could either take I-75 South and then I-4 East, or I-75 South, then the Turnpike, then I-4 West; either way, he was told, he'd end up in Plant City.

The directions only confused him more. He had been told that Plant City was at the end of I-10; he hadn't anticipated detours, interceptions, changes of plans, and damned himself again for being illiterate. And innumerate. And for being lost. Six hours after leaving Tallahassee, he stopped again to ask for directions. They were in Auburndale. A pickup was parked on the side of the road and the driver, as fate would have it, was Mexican. They exchanged pleasantries.

"Me and my family just drove from Matamoros," Javier's father said. "Well, we're actually from Brownsville," he corrected.

"You looking for work?" The Mexican man asked, although he knew the answer. He had seen many families like this one, hungry, eager and willing to break their backs for peanuts. Families just out of the bush, like Javier's, were his business.

"Sí, Sí. We're going to Plant City. Lots of work there, right?"

Javier's father was about to say that although his boy was fourteen, he was strong like an ox, but the Mexican man interrupted him.

"I've lived in Florida all my life and I can tell you this, I've never heard of Plant City. Not such place around here. But if you want to work, I can help you."

They shook hands on the spot. The old man's voice quivered with gratitude. He followed the Mexican man into the belly of this foreign town. There will be food, shelter and work at his farm, the Mexican man said. The old man felt blessed.

For months, the Mexican man kept Javier's family working in an orange farm without a name. They weren't paid for their work; not in cash, the Mexican said, but in kind, as they didn't pay for either food or shelter. The men slept in trailers that were padlocked from the outside every night after work; the women slept with their children inside a house too small for all of them. Whenever Javier's father asked the boss where Plant City was, he got the same *Plant City? Never heard of it.* One Sunday morning, the work camp was woken up by a raucous, drunken boss. The Mexican man stumbled across the camp as he fondled two senoritas that he had brought to keep him company. The alcohol must have made him feel handsome and generous because on a whim, he opened the trailers and told the workers they could go to the flea market if they wanted to. No, they couldn't take their wives along. Just in case they were tempted to run away, the Mexican man said. "I'm drunk, not stupid."

That morning while in *la pulga,* Javier's father ran into other Mexicans. They knew where Plant City was. It was a strawberry-producing town a short drive away from Auburndale. Everybody knew that. And was he stupid? Plant City was not on the beach. He must have heard wrong. That's all he needed to hear. Together with his newly found friends, Javier's father devised an escape plan. No, he wouldn't wait until the next weekend. He'd run away with his family that very night while the Mexican man was still drunk and sandwiched between the two *señoritas.* They agreed to park their van outside the gates and exchange flashlight signals to communicate with one another. The old man would gather his family and run towards the gate, towards freedom, without looking back. They'd leave with what they had on. No time or room to pack the only wedding picture they had, or Javier's baby teeth which his mother turned into a necklace, or their truck, or the crucifix that had hung in the middle of their bedroom in Brownsville.

"And that's what they did," Laura says, before she blows the horn of her van. We are parked outside a sad looking house, green with mold, with broken windows and a collection of rusty old bicycles piled up in the front yard. I don't know where we are. I got lost in her story about Javier and forgot that we were picking up Juanita, the woman without a car.

"Did they ever go back to confront the Mexican man?"

"For what? Where have you heard of people wanting to go back to jail after they escape from it? *'tas loca!*"

Laura points at a pregnant woman coming out of a trailer.

"Look at her, look at her. I keep telling her that she needs to bind her legs together at night with a sheet. Either that or get rid of the damn bed. I'm telling you, that woman is a baby machine."

Juanita, a round and short Mayan-looking woman, walks with little penguin strides.

"*Buenas.*"

"*Buenas,*" Juanita says, wiping off drops of sweat on her forehead. She slides closed the door of the van, and we ride in silence to a produce packing house in Dover.

It's seven a.m. The workers trickle one by one into the packing house located in one corner of a tomato farm. Some of them live on the farm grounds in trailers tucked away into the fields, out of sight from the road. A number of them look sleepy and have crusty eyes and pillow marks, like scars, on their faces. They have magnetic cards that carry basic information about them: a name, probably not the real one, the number of hours worked each day, probably not the real one either, and some other jumbled tidbits of personal information that nobody can decipher.

The workers, most of whom are women, line up and show their cards to the supervisor. Most of them say something that sounds like "morning," but he doesn't reply or make eye contact. He clocks them in with a magnetic receiver and one by one the workers turn on their heels and head to a table with paper hats and disposable gloves. The scene resembles a Holy Communion ritual: the solemnity of the moment, the procession, the offering, the acceptance, the determination as they silently walk to the conveyor belt, the pews.

Laura hands me a magnetic card with someone else's name on it.

"Get in the line and act like a Carmen," she says between her teeth. I'm an impostor; I can't help but feel mischievous. I grin, but Laura tells me with a frown that the situation is anything but humorous.

I clock in as Carmen Toro. The supervisor, a young American man, doesn't even look at me. He doesn't know that I'm not Carmen Toro, or if he does, he doesn't seem to care. All he cares about is the cheap, reliable labor that my hands provide him. Whether these are Carmen's, Perla's, or Lola's hands is irrelevant. I'm a pair of hands and a name tag, not a woman.

Selecting which tomatoes make it to the Americans' tables is a long, tedious, mind-numbing business. In the middle of this monumental building and a few feet from the main door that looks over the tomato fields is a narrow, waist-high conveyor belt about fifteen feet long. The tomatoes are dumped from a funnel-shaped mouth onto a wider conveyor belt that goes around the central one. Workers are positioned on both sides of the outer belt and assigned one of two tasks depending on how far from the tomato-feeding end they are. If they're on one side of the feeder, their job is to get rid of the blemished tomatoes; if they're on the opposite side, their job is to hand-pick whatever color tomato the supervisor shouts for and place it onto the middle band.

I am the fifth one after the feeder and have a few seconds to imitate what the four women before me do. Laura is across the conveyor belt from me, *claseando*, picking colors. Juanita works in silence next to her. She looks shorter and more fragile now that she stands by Laura. Juanita's belly puts an uncomfortable distance between the belt and her hands. She reaches out, arms outstretched in the air. I don't have to see her feet to realize that she stands of her tiptoes. I wonder how long she'll have to endure this discomfort.

There is fear in the air. The women look discreetly over their shoulders as if trying to keep the supervisor in sight. I'm not sure what to fear, but I also feel intimidated. We work in silence, heads down, eyes focused on the hundreds, thousands, maybe millions of tomatoes that the feeder dumps before our hands. We dispose of imperfect tomatoes, whether they're outright rotten, which is unusual, or are slightly blemished. The same group of tomatoes I sort has already been sorted by the eight hands to my right and is further sorted by the remaining thirty hands to my left. Never before had it occurred to me that we in America ate such a refined product, such highly selected and cared-for vegetables. Never before had I realized how utterly spoiled American taste buds are.

The supervisor walks around, radio in hand, taking orders from his distribution centers. Everything works based on demand. He shouts "red," his middleman man shouts "*rojo*" and the women working opposite me transfer red tomatoes rolling on the outer band onto the inner band that ends in the agile hands of an old Mexican man: the packer. The supervisor shouts "red," "orange," "yellow," and his second man shouts "*maduro*," "*naranja*," "*verde*."

After the first hour of standing up in the same position with head cast down, my neck starts to hurt. I look around. Surely, I'll be able to catch a trick or two from the other women to withstand the immobility-induced pain of legs and neck. They stand still like loyal soldiers, even Juanita who hasn't stopped sweating. I switch my weight on the right leg, then the left, then on both. My neck makes a crackling sound every time I look up.

"You like being Carmen?" Laura's voice breaks the silence. Juanita laughs through her fluttering nostrils.

"Who's Carmen anyway?" I ask Laura.

"Oh, so many questions, so little time, *niña*." I hear more constrained laughter.

Laura doesn't look up when she talks. Her eyes, like everybody else's, are fixed onto the little red quivering vegetables on the conveyor belt. I think red: tomatoes, Laura's menses, Juanita's umbilical cord, my own blood and that of those women around me. Rivers of dark red matter running through our veins as we sort millions of red cherry tomatoes.

The bands stop. The noise of the machines is replaced with the voices of the workers who step down their working platforms. Laura tells me that every two hours the *bolillo* gives us ten minutes to rest. We move to the back of the warehouse where there's a vending machine that hasn't been restocked in months and a couple of broken picnic tables. I sit next to Juanita and ask her how she's doing. She is pale under the film of sweat wrapping her plump face. She pats my arm and tells me that she is fine, for the grace of God. Her hand is cold and damp.

"Is it a boy or a girl?" I ask Juanita. She doesn't know. She'll wait and see; hopefully it'll be a boy. She doesn't want more girls. "A woman suffers from the moment she sees her first light," Juanita says, and the other women nod in agreement. Although she is about eight months along with her fourth child, she hasn't visited the doctor since the day she found out she was pregnant. There was something wrong with the shape of her uterus, and the doctor recommended rest. Juanita shakes her head. If she stays home *resting*, she tells me, who pays the seventy-five dollars a week for the trailer she shares with a couple, and the fifteen dollars a day she pays a neighbor to watch over her other three children while she works, and the forty dollars a month for her mobile phone, and the money she is still paying to the coyote who brought her to the USA? And if she stays home *resting,* how does she get the money for diapers and soap and tortillas and milk? And how the hell is she going to bail her husband out of jail if she does as the doctor recommended?

"Why is he in jail?" I ask.

"Because *la poli* pulled him over." Juanita wipes her forehead. She sounds out of breath even though she hasn't moved any body part other than her mouth and hands. "'Cause he had no driver's license. And how the hell is he going to have one if he doesn't have a Social Security number? Huh? You tell me, because I can't understand this country." Everybody around Juanita wholeheartedly agrees. This country *es un país muy loco,* and the system is equally *loco,* and the laws are all *locas.* America and its rules are like a car seen from underneath, one woman says, or like a beggar's hair: all matted, another adds, or like the inside of a radio transistor: outright impossible to understand.

The Living Wage Estimator created by the Poverty in America Project indicates that for a family of four in Plant City, Florida, where a full-time working individual (2080 hours per year) is the sole provider, the living wage per hour is $19.46. This is more than three times Juanita's salary, without taking into account that due to the seasonal nature of her work, she is far from working the 2080 benchmark hours. This reality is far from being unique to Juanita or Plant City. In Hispanic agricultural communities, families working in low-wage jobs make insufficient income to live locally given the local cost of living. The Living Wage Estimator also indicates that Juanita would need to earn a gross annual income of $40,485 to support her family, a far cry from the less than $10,000 a year that she and her husband pull together. Their situation is a common denominator across Hispanic farming communities: The prevailing wage offered by the agricultural sector is not enough to meet minimum standards of living.

"But for the grace of God, I'm much better than my cousin. *Ay, la sonsa.*" A murmur of " *ay, si, si,*" "*pobrecita,*" and "*tan floja,*" runs down the dusty wooden table. Juanita's cousin came to work at the packing house yesterday but had to go home. She is still weak from the ten-day long trek across the border, her feet blistered, her legs bruised, her knees scalded from crawling her way into Texas. Yesterday, she lasted one hour, maybe less, the women tell me. She stood at the platform, her head following the trajectory of the conveyor belt, making a long invisible ellipse with her chin; her world spun and whirled down an imaginary funnel with psychedelic hues of red.

"Don't look at the belt or you'll get dizzy. Pick one spot on the band and wait for the tomatoes to get there," Juanita whispered to her from across the band. The cousin did as Juanita said but couldn't master the technique fast enough. She took a good tug at the woman next to her, but the woman shook her off, commanding her to a get a grip on herself. Juanita told her to sit down and forget about *clasiar* tomatoes, but her cousin insisted. She hadn't earned a penny in weeks. Her children were in Mexico waiting for her to send some money. No, she had to try. But try as she might, she couldn't overcome the dizzying effect of the rotation of the band. She went pale, her lips lost color, her vision got blurry, and then, as if assaulted by a melancholic monster inside her, she quietly vomited a yellow bile into the container of rotten tomatoes. She felt slightly better as the liquid rushed up to her mouth, but the *bolillo* caught her in the act of vomiting and sent her home for good.

I seize the moment and inquire about a woman I know has also suffered enormously. "Does any of you know a woman called Esperanza Vasquez?" I ask. They shake their heads, shrug their shoulders, grin at each other. I have asked a funny question.

"No, but if we find her, don't worry, we'll tell her that Carmen Toro is looking for her," one of the women shouts at me over the *bolillo's* voice that announces our ten-minute break is up.

We put back on the paper hats and the rubber gloves and assume our positions. The conveyor belt starts to rotate, and the tomatoes reverberate as they come out of the funnel. I can't find any blemishes; the tomatoes look unsullied and edible, as if the belt was moving in reverse and we are sorting out the same pile of tomatoes we had just done. The other women keep tossing tomatoes into the waste baskets; I wonder what they are seeing that I don't. I suspend my open hands over the belt ready to dispose of the next blemished one, but the *bolillo* catches me in the act and thinks I'm not working. He walks fast towards me, radio in hand, and positions himself right behind me. I can feel on my neck the hot air coming out of his nostrils. He slips his hand under my right arm and shows me what I need to do at the band. His hand is uncomfortably close to my right breast. I move away to the left.

"You want to work or not?" he asks me. I look at him over my shoulder. He is younger than most of us, has blue eyes, thin pink lips, a broad pale face, peachy skin, ash-colored hair, and a deep dimple of his chin à la Brad Pitt. He is a good-looking man, probably the son of a wealthy rancher who is most likely the son of another wealthy farmer. There is a Hummer parked outside the packing house; I'm sure it's his. It's got a NASCAR sticker paying tribute to Dale Earnhardt.

His radio crackles. He walks away shouting over the radio that hands are particularly fucking slow today, and I know he is referring to mine.

With the supervisor out of sight, I slouch a bit and look around to see if the others are also stretching. They're not. On the contrary, their hands move faster, more expeditiously than before. No one wants the *bolillo* breathing on their necks; no one wants to be blacklisted or labeled as lazy or slow. I feel an uncomfortable wall of silence around me. I want to ask Juanita how she's doing; she has stepped down from the little platform that elevates the workers a foot or so off the floor, and now she looks even shorter than before. I can see only her face sticking over the conveyor. She hasn't stopped sweating.

I look up. Laura stands still, her hands on her hips, chest out, mouth halfway open. It looks like something is gradually welling up inside her. She sucks the air slowly and I imagine that either her esophagus is opening up or that her diaphragm is about to burst. Then she unburdens. She belches like a steam train. Proudly, loudly. I stop working and stare at her in disbelief. Never before have I seen anyone burp with the same shameless fanfare as Laura has done. "*Laura, tu eres tremenda*," the woman next to me says. There are constrained chuckles and snorting noises. Everybody wants to laugh out loud. "*Laura, deja de relajiar que nos van a correr,* don't make us laugh, you're going to get us fired," another woman says, her breasts bouncing over the belt, her face red with swallowed laughter. She looks like she is in pain.

Juanita nudges Laura with her elbow. "What the hell did you eat?"

"Same as you, *manita,* tortillas with fried beans." Laura says, before she lets out yet another more raucous belch.

The other women laugh; they shake their heads, amused and amazed at the same time.

"I've only heard things like that coming out of my husband's mouth and asshole," Juanita says.

The *bolillo* has stepped outside the packing house. The women don't stop working but are now laughing and commenting on Laura's explosion.

"I think it's a man thing, this farting and burping like we feed them dynamite," Juanita says between chuckles. "A woman doesn't make those noises. Everything about a woman is more delicate. Even her farts smell different. Like roses."

"Speak for yourself, *manita.* You should smell mine. My farts are *de madre!* I even scare the shit out of our poor Chihuahua," Laura says. I laugh hard and so does everyone left and right. In the midst of our explosion of giggles and snorts, it dawns on me that Laura's comment is not that funny; it's a mere tension reliever. We laugh because the *bolillo* is not watching, because we've been tense for too long, because we're tired, and hungry, and because laughing makes us feel human and alive again.

Two hours, later we have our second break. Men and women who've been planting strawberries and picking tomatoes join us at the packing house. They're easy to identify. They're sunburned, their clothes dirty, their hands green from the tomato foliage; they're sweaty and hot.

One of the newcomers sees his *compadre* sitting at the picnic table next to mine.

"*Orale, tu, pinche buey,*" he says.

"*Que? Pinche puto cabrón?*" the *compadre* replies.

Insults taken care of, they grin, shake hands, and share a bottle of 7-Up.

"How much are you getting paid today?" I ask Laura.

"Minimum wage," she says, as she ties her shoelaces.

"$6.15 per hour?" I ask.

"No, six dollars. Where did you get the other fifteen from?"

"It's the law," I say. "Minimum wage was raised in Florida last November from $5.15 to $6.15 per hour."

"Maybe the *bolillo* doesn't know. He hasn't said anything." Laura says. Her right foot is on the bench, and her generous breasts hang loosely on each side of her right knee.

"And anyway, fifteen cents buys you nothing. Only a fool would whine over fifteen *pinche* cents."

I explain to Laura that's beside the point. It's not what fifteen cents more can buy; it's the law. It's what she is entitled to. Minimum wage is a set number, not a guideline.

"You need to tell him." I say, but I mean, she needs to let him know that she knows.

When the shift is over, I plunge myself into the passenger's seat of Laura's van and scribble in my notebook: "These women are far from being broken by hardship. They are as vibrant and alive as anyone else. If the rest of the world is looking at them with pity and condescension, the world is seriously misled." Sure, they'd have preferred to be somewhere else, most likely Mexico, but they were proud to be working a decent job, supporting their families back at home where work is scarce and minimum wage is a concept unheard of. So they make the best of it, stealing pleasure from every possible moment.

And if, as indicated by the Poverty in America Project, the minimum wage for this county is seventy-four percent below the living wage rate and the local poverty level is fifty-two percent below the national poverty level, these women don't know it. These facts and figures mean nothing to them. To them poverty is not what happens when their salary is way below an officially pre-established number. Poverty is what makes a pregnant woman with a deformed uterus stand on her feet for eight or ten hours a day; poverty is what propels a woman to show up for work two days after crossing the desert on foot; poverty is eating, day in and day out, a couple of cold tortillas for lunch. Poverty is working under fear, fear of awaking the boss's wrath. God's wrath. Fear of having hands that are *particularly fucking slow* one day and being asked not to come back, or denied work the following day. Poverty is the realization of one's irrelevance and disposability.

Griselda

A couple of months after working with Laura, I'm back in the strawberry fields. This time in Seffner, a small town located sixteen miles east of downtown Tampa. Yesterday, after yet another wild-goose chase after Esperanza, I was approached by Griselda, a farmworker who had heard rumors about my quest. She said she was too tired to talk but that she'd tell me all about Esperanza if I came back today and give her a hand in the field.

"All I'm telling you today is that she is in Perry," Griselda said.

I went home exhilarated, hopeful. I located Perry on the map: a four hour drive from Lakeland. I could find a small hotel room and interview her over a few days. A simple task with high probabilities of success. Under the comfort of my sheets and in the safety of my home, I reinvented Esperanza overnight. In the dark, my imagined Esperanza was younger than ever before, had a mouthful of perfect teeth and lips that smiled widely and often. She was taller than my other Esperanzas and had a monumental behind that made men weak in the knees. She spoke Spanish with an American accent and sang Mexican *cumbias*. People everywhere called her *Reina*. Jesus Christ. Last night I fell asleep thinking that Esperanza looked like Selena Perez, the queen of Tejano music.

This field is a vast scatter of bright specks. Ripe strawberries lie across the plot of land in a thick layer of crimson punctuated by the green foliage above and the black soil underneath it. The sky hangs high, awhirl with a hundred shades of blue. From a distance, it looks like an Impressionist canvas in full frenzy. I think it's the spring morning light that illuminates the field with a sort of surreal radiance, or maybe the rays of hope that came with the news I have just heard from Griselda, that Esperanza might be living in Pierson, the fern capital of the world. I must have gotten Pierson and Perry mixed up.

The plants are thick and now with the substantial foliage, the space between the rows is even narrower than it was during planting. We are forced to squat sideways, our thighs parallel to the bed but our torsos and head twisted facing the fruit. It's a grueling position to work in. After a few minutes of squatting, I switch to a kneeling pose. Squat, kneel, pick, pack, move forward, repeat. We look like entrenched soldiers moving down the field in full crouch, dragging our knees, forming a thin ditch with the tip of our shoes as we move our bodies from plant to plant.

We have just started and I'm already falling behind Griselda. I thought that picking strawberries was going to be easier than planting them. But, I'm wrong. Again. I don't know how she does it. It takes her a few seconds to fill the plastic one-pound containers with the produce. So much for unskilled labor.

"*Echale ganas, manita!*" she urges me, looking at me over her shoulder. "Between the two of us we can make 200 boxes today. *Orale, no te rajes!*" She hurls innocent insults at me and calls me every variation of wimp she can think of: chicken, *mimada*, sissy, *floja*.

"Andale, the slave master is paying $1.50 per box," she says referring to the crew leader as *negrero*.

"Three hundred dollars for a day's work? Are you serious? That's fantastic," I shout, excited. Men and women working the other rows scoff, tsk-tsk, and a few of them shake their heads without facing me.

"Three hundred dollars a day?" Griselda asks, dumping a handful of gigantic strawberries into the plastic container. "*'Tas loca?* That's more than a week's work," she corrects. "I said $1.50 per box, but not this *chinga* little thing," she says pointing at the green basket. "I mean this one." Griselda throws a few cardboard boxes at me.

"You put eight of these little plastic baskets inside the big cardboard box and that's called a flat, that's what the *bolillo* pays at $1.50."

Last week I went to the grocery store and paid $1.75 for one pound of strawberries. How could the worker get paid the same amount for supplying eight pounds? Where does the eightfold increase in price come from? The same flat for which the picker gets paid $1.50 in the field is sold a few hours later at $10 in the supermarket.

I ask her if she knows how much a pound of strawberries cost in Wal-Mart, where I know she shops once in a while. No, she doesn't know the price of anything in *Gualma*, Wal-Mart. She buys only beans, tortillas, and sodas, maybe a whole chicken if she can afford it, but other than that, she doesn't know and she doesn't care.

"Whether food is cheap or expensive, *me vale madre*." She doesn't give a fuck.

Griselda uses her index finger to press shut one nostril and blows hard through the other. I see light rain, like a sprinkle, come out of her nose. She is short, stout, and masculine. From a distance, she looks like a man, with her baggy jeans, loose-fitting shirts, and a sideways baseball cap with the words LA RAZA embroidered in the colors of the Mexican flag. She is a ferocious looking woman with a permanent derisive smirk and scrutinizing eyes that seem to see it all.

She closes another container until its corners make a clicking sound, shakes it, then opens it again. There is still room for another strawberry. The crew leaders are particular about how the strawberries are packed, she explains. The container has to be shaken to allow the strawberries to settle naturally in a fit that can't be too snug or too tight. If there is still room, an extra strawberry is selected. This selection requires swift eyes and judgment for if the extra unit is too big, the plastic cover ends up squashing it when shut closed.

"Just *one*, did you hear that? He finds *one* blemished strawberry and that's it," Griselda says. "He doesn't pay us for the whole basket." He keeps the basket, replaces the blemished fruit himself with an unsullied one, but the worker doesn't get paid for it. "Memorize that," she instructs me. "You write it down like I'm telling you, okay?"

I don't know why I'm on edge around Griselda. I can't put my finger on it. Maybe it's the way she keeps tabs on the number of baskets I gather, maybe it's the little smirk with which she ends every story, maybe it's the malice of the gossip she tells me about other women working alongside us. I'm thinking about this when she starts to laugh. She tells me that she just remembered something funny and do I want to hear it? I have no option and say, "Sure."

She tells me that three months after she gave birth to her only child, she got into a *battle* with her husband.

"What was the fight about?" I ask her.

"Are you listening to me?" she says. "I didn't say fight, did I? I said *battle*. Get this *chinga* story right so you don't go around telling people lies about me," Griselda adds as she shakes another basket full of strawberries.

He pushed her against the wall of their trailer; in return, she grabbed the iron and swung the electric cord, hitting him in the eye with the plug. Her husband lost his balance and fell on his rear end. Griselda charged him, iron in hand. He crawled under the table, both hands covering his bleeding eye, but Griselda picked him by his hair, dragged him out of the trailer, threw him onto the street, and pummeled his face bloody with the heel of a shoe.

"I had already warned him that I had more *huevos* than any man. I told him that if he ever roughed me up, I'd show him who was the man of the house." Griselda packs strawberries at a furious pace; I'm getting the hang of it and start closing the gap between the two of us. I crawl down the row until my knees touch the soles of her sandals.

"I grew up homeless on the streets of Mexico City. Imagine a little girl alone in Mexico? *Heeeeeeh.*" Griselda's hands dance around the strawberry plants. She finds the perfect fruits without even looking, yanks them out, keeps the green leaf hat on them which makes the fruit last longer, packs them, seals the box. Snap, click.

"I never went to school but I can count and read and write my name. I might be *chiquita* and *feíta,* a little short and a little ugly, but I tell you this, nobody messes with me. That's why people call me *Malinche*. It's not that I don't like other Mexicans, it's them that don't like me."

Griselda stops for a second and turns her head to face me, dry snot resting on her septum, and arches her untamed eyebrows as she tells me that the rumors about her are not true. "*No soy ni puta ni marimacha,*" she's neither a whore nor a lesbian. "They're just jealous because I work as hard as everybody but I always have extra *chavos*. It's pure envy."

Scorned and publicly humiliated by his wife, Griselda's husband went to the police to accuse Griselda of beating their baby. She tells me that a representative from Children and Families came to their trailer with her husband and demanded to see the baby. When the representative explained the accusations, Griselda lost her temper and punched her husband in the face. She was charged on the spot with domestic violence. Two days later, Social Services came to take the baby away from Griselda.

The months that followed were hazy and filled with contained tears, anger and contempt for men, the American system, herself, everything. The police visits got her evicted from the trailer and she ended up renting a corner in an over-crowded trailer full of men. She slept with a pocketknife in her hand. For protection, she says. The men knew how short tempered and quick with the knife she was. No one dared to touch Griselda. She managed to convince Children and Families that she was a fit mother and eventually they returned the baby to her, by which time she had become a heavy drinker. Two months after mother and baby were reunited, a social worker spotted inebriated Griselda walking down the streets with the baby in her arms. She lost the baby once again, this time for good.

The wind blows some of my empty boxes, forming a fast-moving tornado. The crew leader shouts angry *hey, hey, hey's* at me. I jump over the fruit-filled rows catching the boxes in the air, on the ground, on other workers' backs. I feel useless and inadequate.

"I thought you were going to help me," Griselda complains. "You're more trouble than help," she says.

She is beginning to wind me up and my patience is thinning rapidly. I'm not sure I'll last until the field is clean. I take a risk.

"Where did you meet Esperanza?" I ask.

"Esperanza?" she looks up at a passing plane, then grins. "Have you ever thought about why we name women like that? Esperanza, Caridad, Concepción, Piedad. That tells you something, you know what I mean?" she asks and moves faster ahead of me.

I'm not interested in discussing why so many Latinas are named Hope, Charity, Conception, or Piety. I want to know about Esperanza. I wonder if maybe she knows that I'm looking for her and hasn't been able to find me. I wonder if right now she is also on edge, tired, and being bossed around by another *Malinche*.

At the end of the day we have picked fifteen flats, each containing eight plastic one-pound containers. We worked nine hours, picked 120 pounds of strawberries, and made $22.50. A few hours later, our effort will be sold for $180 at the supermarkets.

"I'm sorry I wasn't very good at this," I say to Griselda after she hands our tokens to the crew leader.

"That's exactly what I'll tell my landlord when he comes around to collect the rent," Griselda retorts.

I take a bandana out of my pocket and wipe my forehead, my neck, my upper lip. I can taste the salt of my sweat. We are leaning against an old pickup that Griselda got from an admirer. "The fruit of a love transaction," she says.

"He said that he liked me, that he was lonely and needed some company. I told him I liked him too, and that I was tired of riding a *baica* and I needed a car." She sticks her right hand inside her shirt and under her left arm. She rubs her armpit, pulls her hand out, and takes a sniff before wiping her sweaty hand on the sleeves of her jeans. "I don't give unless I can take," Griselda adds. "You have to be like that or you get eaten alive."

She takes off her baseball cap to scratch her scalp. Her hair is turning white on one spot of her head. Lightning bolts seem to fire down her short and greasy rope of hair. Griselda forms a sluggish four with her legs—right shin folded in front of the left—puts her baseball cap back on, back to front, tucks her hands in the pockets of her jeans (I wonder if she still carries her pocketknife), sucks her teeth, and says that she'd rather make $22.50 picking strawberries than $50 picking tomatoes.

"You fill a bucket with thirty-two pounds of tomatoes, run like hell with that bucket on your shoulder, give it to the man in the truck at the end of the *feel*, he dumps your tomatoes, gives you back the bucket and you run back to your row."

"How much do you get paid for each bucket?"

"*Cuarenta centavos,* forty cents." Griselda looks up. She looks more indigenous now with her face glistening under the sun, her oblique eyes half shut, her cheekbones looking higher than normal at this moment that her nose is screwed into a button.

"That's less than one penny per pound," I think out loud. "A pound of tomatoes is more than a dollar in the supermarket." Griselda reminds me that she knows nothing about prices. All she buys is a pound of *pinche* Maseca flour to make tortillas, Pepsi, beans, and a *pinche* pollo once in a while, if she can afford it. Wasn't I paying attention when she told me?

"How many tomatoes do you have to pick in one day to be able to buy food and pay the rent?" I ask her but immediately realize that this is the wrong question because at the going rate, the amount of tomatoes one needs to pick in one day to survive is beyond what a human being can do. Griselda doesn't give me time to rephrase.

"You have to pick 100 buckets to get forth dollars," Griselda tells me matter-of-factly. I see her with my mind's eye, hauling a thirty-two-pound red bucket on her right shoulder. Her bowed legs buckle with the weight as she walks towards the collection truck. An inverted moon of dry blood, where the bucket sits on her shoulder, touches the right side of her neck with its apex. The protuberant bone on her shoulder girdle has been blistered, healed, blistered over, healed again, and finally turned into a callous cushion of dead skin. The skin there is so hard that she could be shot on that spot without feeling pain.

"Then you go home with your hands all green and coughing and scratching all over because of the medicine," Griselda says, interrupting the mental picture.

"Which medicine?"

"The medicine the *bolillos* use to kill bugs. All these *tomateras* are sprayed with medicine."

"You mean chemicals?" I ask Griselda. Instead of answering she walks around the pickup to the driver's side and tells me she wants to go home, take a shower, and go downtown to find out how much is a bus ticket to Mexico. She wants to go and visit La Raza, then come back to the USA and make some serious money. I want her to know that immigration laws are about to change and that this is probably not the best time to attempt an illegal entry into the USA. But I know better and don't dare to say a direct word of warning. Instead, I ask her if she's heard about some politicians wanting to criminalize undocumented workers like herself.

"The way people treat me when I go to the *Gualma* or if the police pull me over? I feel already like a criminal."

I decide to press my luck. "Do you know that some people high up want to build 700 miles of fencing along the border?" I quiz Griselda. She stops before opening the door of the pickup and scoops up a bit of dirt with her big right toe. Her toenails are uneven and framed with black dirt outlines.

"That's a good idea," she says as her left hand fiddles with something inside her pocket. I think about the knife again.

"Who do you think is going to end up building it? Us, LA RAZA. See? More jobs for us," she says, clears her throat and spits a thick wad of green phlegm. "I could sell tamales by the wall, feed the workers, take those *güero gringos* for tours. I bet there is a lot of money to be made."

She opens her pickup and sits behind the wheel. I walk around and wait for her to open the passenger's door. She turns the engine on and it revs, then stops. The exhaust coughs up a dry splutter. She looks at me, exasperated, and rolls down the passenger's window, but doesn't open the door.

"*Hijo de tu pinche madre,*" I hear her say, brooding and swearing at the car. She starts the pickup again, and this time it revs with power. It's painfully apparent that Griselda has no desire to talk to me. Before she puts the pickup into gear, I ask her where exactly in Pierson I can find Esperanza.

"Which Esperanza?" Griselda asks, looking me straight in the eye. My heart sinks.

"Esperanza Vasquez," I say. "You told me that if I helped you out in the field today, you'd tell me where to find her. Remember?"

Griselda sucks her teeth, the beginning of a sneer forming in one corner of her mouth.

"Oooh, tsk. You didn't tell me it was *Vasquez*," Griselda mumbles as she flicks the dry snot off her nose. "I thought you said Esperanza, umm, Rodriguez."

I take a long lungful of air and let out a sigh of frustration. "That's OK, Griselda. Don't worry about it." I send a mound of dust whirling up in the air with an angry kick of my shoe. I've been duped. She had heard that I helped farmworkers in the fields in exchange for information, and she had played me like a violin. I'm tired, hungry, frustrated, and in pain. An old injury in my right shoulder which I've kept at bay with Ibuprofens has come back to full spasm-strength today. Or maybe not. Maybe it's always been there, but the extraordinary bond that I've formed with the other farmworker women before Griselda has had the palliative effect of a placebo.

I can't be stern with Griselda, as embittered and as fond of trickery as she is. Extra *chavos* or not, she is undocumented, voiceless, and poor. Crushingly poor. And poverty, I've seen, and the misfortunes it brings along with it are great character modifiers. Poverty hardens women, especially mothers who develop into ferocious beings willing to do anything to get a little extra for themselves and their children. I've witnessed powerful transformations throughout the years of field work among women; the tamest become sly, the most uneducated conniving, their relentlessness growing exponentially with the number of children. Their transgressions range from lining up twice or more at charity giveaways to selling in their front yards the goods they receive free of charge at parochial distribution centers. They, it could be said, are the venture capitalists of the poor.

Griselda's truck disappears in a mushroom of loose dust, like a devil's whirl. That's her world, an impenetrable fortress of solitude and anger. It is a darkness disguised as resilience, misfortune veiled with pride. Both equally damning, equally tragic.

By the time I get behind the wheel, the farmworkers have already left. I look left and right and realize that I have no idea where I am. That I don't know which way is the interstate. That I'm thirsty, hungry, sore and in desperate need of a shower. I turn the ignition on and before I put the car in drive I let out a colorful string of curse words.

The Wetbacks Are Coming
A Manifesto

The wetbacks are coming. You can see them all the way from Tucson, Arizona. They run and slither and crouch like animals. They emerge from the desert covered in dust. Crusty eyes; ashy, matted hair; shredded clothes; dry mucus on their children's noses. They look deranged. They cross the border with bloody hands and scraped knees. Blood doesn't scare them. They are the living descendants of Mayan kings and Aztec princesses who practiced human sacrifice to appease their gods. Their ancestors laid the offering on a stone slab at the center of their temple, cut right through her abdomen, extracted her beating heart and threw the decapitated body down the temple stairs. And as she crosses the line, you can see all of this in her face because wetback women have eloquent bodies. Everything is recorded on their flesh. A quick glance and you can tell that they spent their nights under Crucifixion Thorn trees, the barbs of the cactus still lodged in their calloused feet. It doesn't hurt them. They look human but they have dragon feet.

Look at the fresh wetbacks. They come out of the water half naked, their hair slick with river bacteria. Leeches feed off their scrawny flesh, their legs are imprinted with the sharp edges of underwater rocks. Hungry hordes of them cross the river in inflatable tubes the color of tar. You can spot them from McAllen, Texas. Heaps of short, brown-skin tadpoles coming ashore, their gills filled with river mud. They're hungry, thirsty, always, and will eat what's stale and drink what's filthy without compunction. Every day is D day. A new Omaha beach this side of the Rio Bravo.

They're nocturnal creatures. Study them through your night vision goggles. They are red foxes. They double back on their own tracks in an attempt to confuse you, their main predator. Don't they look like raccoons with those black patches under their eyes? Zoom in on them. Stay there, be patient. They play possum when chased. One minute they lie there, still, not blinking, their patchy tongues hanging out of their chapped mouths; the next minute they're gone. Get closer to the fence, they are badgers. They have long, curved claws which they use to poke around in the dirt for food or burrow their way into your kitchen.

Beware. They are closely related to skunks, martens and weasels in that they are omnivores and will eat anything they can bury their teeth in: rodents, frogs, snakes, worms, fruits, and roots. They'll devour your pantry, and when they're done, they'll chew on its mahogany shelves and its silver handles. Scan the horizon west to east and back. They are margays. They have binocular vision and are skillful climbers. See them trampling each other like wildebeest as they go over the fence. Remarkably agile, aren't they? Their ankles can turn up to 180 degrees and are able to jump up to twelve feet horizontally while carrying their offspring on their backs.

Wetback women make a lot of noise. They can be heard from Mexicali, California. You can hear the crucifixes around their necks rattling against their rosaries, and the rosaries clattering against the images of the Virgen de Guadalupe, and the Virgin's rays of light clanking noisily with the wind. When they whisper their prayers, you can hear the hum from San Diego all the way to the Redwood Forest. Even the wooden scapulars bursting with text and images howl in the night; one square on the chest, the other dropped down their backs. You should see what they do before they come. They make the pilgrimage to Los Altos de Jalisco to pray at the tomb of Saint Toribio Romo, the patron saint of the wetbacks. They bring offerings: chickens, goats, cigarettes, tequila and crates of Coca-Cola, and in exchange, they ask for a successful crossing and a safe journey back home. Then they sing.

Look at the wetbacks on the interstate outside Las Cruces, New Mexico. Twenty of them crammed in a van with tinted windows and no A/C. The seats have been removed to make space for the human cargo. They haven't bathed in weeks and the van reeks of sweat and menstrual blood. They lie on the floor of the vehicle, wriggling like worms. Their intertwined legs cramp up, their necks twitch, their backs throb. One gets motion-sick and vomits gelatinous green bile; another passes out from exhaustion and indignity, and both go unnoticed.

Take a look at them toiling in the fields on the outskirts of your town. They have no shame. They arrive barefoot and hungry and within hours they are already working in farms across the country. Their feet still oozing pus from the desert crossing, their hands still bleeding memories of razor barbed wire and cacti. Know that they will have touched everything you put in your mouth. Fruits and vegetables, everything bulbous, everything that sprouts and nourishes, everything with peels and seeds and sheaths and edible flesh.

Since their arrival, stooping has become their most natural posture. Look at their children working in the field, with their dexterous little hands and quick feet; look at the pregnant women bent at the waist, their fetuses tucked in one corner of their wombs while they toil and get bathed in pesticides.

They come with their dangerous names: Rodriguez and Ramirez and Restrepo and Rita and Guillermina and Gregoria. Names that expect your tongue to engage in impossible muscle acrobatics. "R's" so strong that they make your palate sore and your tonsils sting for days. Don't bother. Call them Pepe and Pancha, they'll smile all the same, grateful that you care to call them anything at all. Their children can be a little bit trickier. Some women give them indigenous names so that they don't forget where they come from: Axochitl, Xochimitl, Itzamatul, Ix Chel and Yatzil, which means, The Loved One, in Maya.

Slow your truck down as you drive by a grove and you'll hear, not them, they don't talk much, but their music. They listen to dodgy songs: violent border *corridos*, playful *Norteños*, heart-wrenching *mariachis*, sleazy *Duranguenses* and Tex-Mex *cumbias* played with dissonant accordions that make you want to rub your hips against someone else's. You won't understand a word; the only discernable thing in their music is the lamentations: *Ayayayayyyyy!*

Wetback women are highly adaptable. They are more than happy to share with another ten compatriots a condemned trailer with broken windows. You see, they like fresh air. They sleep on the floor on moldy mattresses and pay no mind to cockroaches nibbling at their toes. Cockroaches are like pets for them. They even have a song dedicated to this insect; it's called La Cucaracha. In those overcrowded trailers, they live on tortillas made with Maseca flour and salsas *picosas* that would sear your esophagus. They go to flea markets shopping for tacky outfits which they take back to their trailer where they celebrate *quinceañera* parties, baptisms, first communions, confirmations, and birthday piñatas. They have it good in this country.

Pay attention to your salad, focus on that strawberry while you chocolate-fondue it, feel the slippery roundness of those watermelon seeds you leisurely spit on your beautifully manicured lawn, look at the spotless toilet in a public restroom, and ponder. Who makes possible the crispy lettuce, the juicy cucumbers, the unblemished peach, the perfect hedgerows in your yard shielding you from the world? Now think about a particular group of women you have seen: short, sunburned, fleshy midriffs, flat hips, saggy breasts all tucked up in skin-tight blue jeans and promotional shirts. And ponder some more.

If you find yourself stuck in traffic because they are parading downtown, heaps of children in tow, like this is their own country, asking for fair pay, rights, and immigration amnesty, do something. Write to your representatives, to your constituents, your pastor, the pope. Because of the wetbacks' shenanigans you were late picking up your kid from ballet class. What has this country come to? Blow your horn, disrupt their peaceful protest, drive right through the parade. They're blocking the entrance to your gym. How inconvenient!

And if nothing works and your protests go unheeded, go back to the border and patrol it yourself. It's only a 1900-mile stretch. Build a wall of inextinguishable fire, set up posts along the border with venom-spitting dragons, rotate lethal formations of blood sucking bats, position angry cherubs along the fence and train them to release their arrows south-bound, send armies of engineered fireflies to illuminate the perimeter, dig bottomless trenches. Take your pick. But remember, these wetbacks are willful, hungry, thirsty, desperate, and are descendants of Mayan kings and Aztec princesses who practiced human sacrifice. And you'll see all of this in their faces as the cross the border. Again. And again.

Francisca

oday is Carlitos' birthday. We gather at a parochial community hall adja-
cent to the Guadalupe church in Immokalee where an army of case workers have volunteered their culinary skills to celebrate Carlitos' first birthday. It's
a Mexican fiesta. An array of salsas *picosas* and homemade nachos fill the center
of the white vinyl-covered table. Mexican aromas meander through the hall all
the way from the kitchen to the cement benches outside the door. It smells of
fried beans, rice and a medley of pork, chicken and all the edible meats in the
world. Women sit in plastic chairs placed next to each other against the walls.
Some have their babies on their laps; some have them in American-made baby
strollers and car seats. The men stand outside, they don't like to hang around
women and babies. They chat, laugh, and tell jokes in Amusgo, a Mayan dialect
that only they can understand.

The spirits are high, but there is no music, or a piñata, or balloons. There are
no blowouts or cone hats. No lollipops or curling ribbon eggs in coordinated
colors. There can't be any of that. Carlitos is not a regular baby. He was born
without limbs. His body is a perfect rectangle of flesh and bones toppled by
a perfectly round head of soft hair. He giggles a lot, more than a regular baby.
Francisca, his mother, a teenager who screws her nose when she laughs and looks
more like a Mayan doll than the mother of a deformed baby, sits in one corner
of the room with Carlitos glued to her chest with a kangaroo-style baby carrier.
The other Mexican mothers try not to look but can't help themselves; they pry
with morbid curiosity, with pity, with confusion. *How could this happen to an
innocent baby?* one asks. *Maybe someone gave the mother the evil eye when she was
pregnant*, another woman comments.

The party guests have been carefully chosen. They are farmworkers from the
community, mainly from Guerrero, the same Mexican state that Carlitos' parents are from and they all have babies. Sick babies. The unspoken theme of the
party is solidarity. The case workers want Francisca and her husband to feel that
they are not alone, that other mothers have also given birth to extraordinary

babies like Carlitos and that this is a safe place where the deformed, the under-developed, the handicapped, the feeble are all beautiful children.

Across the dinner table from me is Cristina. She smiles at me while chewing warm tortillas with a mouthful of silver-jacketed teeth. Her shiny black hair is gathered on the back of her head with a braid so tight that it makes her brown eyes slant a bit. She looks Mongolian. Juanito, her baby, is five months old and like Carlitos, he is no ordinary baby. He was born with cleft lip and palate and some other issues that if I want, she says, she'll tell me later. Cristina gulps a hungry mouthful of fried bean dip as she motions me to walk around the table.

"Come see my baby," she says.

I accept the invitation. Juanito is asleep inside his stroller. Half of his baby face is at peace; the other half, the one with the cleft, is at war. A deep trench interrupts the course of his upper lip, separating it into left and right. The trench disappears into his left nostril. His mouth is closed, yet I can see his pink tongue somewhere behind the trench.

"Today, I realize how fortunate I'm," Cristina tells me as I caress Juanito's baby face. "At least my son will be able to walk and run and comb his own hair. Not like Carlitos. Look at him. Doesn't it break your heart?" We exchange silent looks, and then she adds, "Maybe the mother didn't go to church when she was pregnant. Is she Catholic?"

This is no ordinary party. There is an American journalist who traveled to the heart of the Mexican mountains to show Francisca's parents pictures of their deformed grandson. Their pain was carefully documented for a series of newspaper articles. Their tears, their disbelief, their confusion. The snapshots taken in the Mexican jungle are worth a fortune in shock value. There is also an intrusive photographer pointing her camera lenses at Carlitos from every possible angle. The woman shoots while Francisca feeds him, when he is standing in a barrel-shaped device with leather straps that allows him to be upright, when he frowns inside his straight-jacket-like apparatus, when he giggles, when he cries, when he spits his food. The photographer doesn't ask for permission; she is a woman on a mission. Francisca and her husband Abraham hold the baby and smile for the camera, once, twice, and many more times until Francisca stops smiling and Abraham leaves the hall to join the other men outside. Young Francisca looks as though if she could have it her way, she'd wrap Carlitos up in a magic blanket and make him disappear from prying lenses and shocked eyes.

In one corner of the hall, with dark bangs covering her eyes and a t-shirt bursting with food stains and dry breast milk circles, is another extraordinary guest. Rosa holds in her arms her three-month old baby, a boy named Camilo.

This happy and healthy looking baby laughs intermittently, staring into space as if some imaginary circus clowns were performing only for his amusement.

"He's a little sick," Rosa tells me when I touch his tiny fingers with mine. "It's a miracle that he is alive," she adds. I'm about to ask her what his problem is but she cradles Camilo in one arm and with the other lifts his shirt. A pink scar divides his baby chest into two.

"Heart problems," she says, "and some other things but not as important as his heart." Rosa shakes her bangs on his face, cooing into his breath. Camilo cooes back.

If a Mexican woman by the name of Sostenes hadn't gone to work to the Carolinas, she would also be at the party with her fourth son, a boy named Jesus. She was Francisca's neighbor and coworker in the Immokalee fields where they picked tomatoes in the same farm. Sostenes left because there was something wrong with Immokalee, either in the water, the food, or the air. She didn't know and she didn't stay to find out. Jesus was born with Pierre Robin Syndrome, a condition in which the lower jaw is exceedingly small, set back, and the tongue is displaced toward the back of the throat. All she knew was that baby Jesus, unlike his three healthy siblings, was at risk of swallowing his own tongue and dying of asphyxiation at any given time. She had never heard of such a thing. It was best to leave Florida just in case she got pregnant again and the air, the water, or the food in Immokalee warped once more the life in her womb.

And had Maria not lost the baby, she would have also been at the party. She lived in the same migrant labor camp and worked for the same produce company as Francisca and Sostenes did. Two months after Carlitos was born, Maria gave birth to an underweight baby boy with no nose, no ears, an under-developed heart, malfunctioning lungs and an impending transformation. He was born a boy, named Jorge, but his underdeveloped genitals looked more like those of a girl and the boy had to be re-named Violeta. Jorge, Violet, died a few days after being born. I'm told that Maria is back in Mexico where nobody in her village has ever given birth to deformed babies.

"Maybe it's the American air," one woman says.

"Maybe it's all that shit that we breathe in the fields," another adds.

Maybe. Then again, maybe not.

And if the Guatemalan woman who lives just across the street from the church hadn't had her toddler lying on a hospital bed, recovering from a liver transplant, she would have also been here today. She would have reminded me that in 2003 one of her other children also needed a liver transplant but didn't qualify for one because of the additional complications with hydrocephaly and respiratory problems. So he died. Had she been here today, she would have most certainly repeated what she told me on the day I drove her to the hospital in Ft. Myers to see her baby: "I gave birth to my eldest in a little village in Guatemala, without doctors or hospitals. You should see her. Strong as an ox," she said, her hands curled into fists. "But the ones born here in this country are made out of eggshells, all weak, like you can break them with a sigh."

When journalists, photographers and camera men and women found out about Carlitos, Francisca and Abraham became local epitomes of what parenthood is all about. Abraham appeared on early pictures with a wide smile of even white teeth and Francisca with her nose screwed into a fleshy button that accentuated her Mayan doll facial traits. They looked happy, resigned and united by the tragic deformity of their first baby.

I've been trying to get an interview with Francisca since the day I met her at Carlitos' birthday party, but locating Francisca or her husband was almost as impossible as finding Esperanza. They, like most of the other farmworkers I've interviewed, constantly change their mobile phone numbers. There is always someone ready to offer an undocumented farmworker an attractive calling plan, a modern flip cellular phone, and an array of eye-catching features for a steep initial fee that promises to shrink to a fraction in a few weeks. The buzz that comes with the flashy flip phone fades away at the end of the first month of usage when the farmworker receives an exorbitant bill that no one in their right mind would pay for a month worth of service. The outcome is standard. The farmworkers leave the bill delinquent (whose credit history is it going to affect if the account holder is undocumented?) and go shopping somewhere else, where there is always someone willing to sell them an even more attractive plan, flashier features, and so the cycle goes.

Farmworkers are also constantly on the move. They live in condemned trailers that have to be vacated over night, or fall behind on rent payments and have to look for cheaper accommodation, or after a harvest is over they are offered work in a different town. They are transient, Hispanic gypsies moving their caravans of dreams across the Floridian fields.

Changes of addresses and telephone numbers were not the only hurdles I had to go over to get to Francisca. With the wave of reporters, photographers, and TV cameras came a group of lawyers, each of whom offered to legally represent the parents of Carlitos, Jorge/Violeta, and Jesús, *los tres niños,* as they are known in Immokalee. The lawyers needed a cluster to initiate a civil lawsuit against the produce farm the three mothers worked for when they were pregnant. But Maria and Sostenes left Florida and the cluster was reduced to a single mother: Francisca. Without the cluster the chances of winning the case were slim. One by one the lawyers disappeared, all but one who out of either compassion or professional greed, or both, decided to lead Francisca through the complicated process of a multimillion lawsuit against her former employer. His legal representation offer came with a small price: confidentiality. Francisca interpreted her lawyer's gag order as a divine prohibition to talk to anyone about anything related to Carlitos, her pregnancy, her life, past, present or future.

When I finally locate her, we have long telephone conversations. No, I can't visit her, she says. She's busy with Carlitos, but will I call her back some other day? She says she likes my Colombian accent. I like her sparse Spanish and how she makes me repeat everything I say.

Her initial reluctance to receive me at her house fades gradually as we get to know each other better. Eventually she agrees to see me. But before she gives me her new address she looks for the last sliver of reassurance.

"You're not a reporter, right?"

"No, I'm not."

"So you don't work for a newspaper or a magazine, *no?*"

"No, I don't."

"You know I can't talk about the lawsuit, right?"

"Yes, I do."

"So, you won't ask?"

"No, I won't."

Francisca comes to the door dressed in a beautiful red *huipil*. Her mother is an artisan, she explains after I compliment the intricate white brocade. Half of her straight, lustrous hair is up in a capricious bun, the other half rains softly over her back. She's barefoot. She's got baby skin, vibrant eyes, small fingers, plump feet with traces of different shades of polish on her toenails, and a constant tilt of the head the way children have when curious or surprised. I have to remind myself that she is not simply a teenager; she is the mother of no other than Carlitos, the baby without limbs.

We sit on a large couch with the baby propped between us. He smiles and gurgles, looking in his mother's direction. His eyes seem more eager and his mouth more avid of spoken words than a regular baby. If Carlitos had arms, he would probably be marveling at the sight of his own hands, grasping and releasing fistfuls of air, drawing invisible shapes into space, tugging at his mother's *huipil*, pressing the flashing buttons of her cellular phone. But he doesn't have arms. Not even stumps long enough to dream of prostheses that might one day embrace Francisca with the robotic hug of an artificial set of arms. Not even that.

Francisca places a reassuring hand on Carlitos' tummy as she starts her story. She was born nineteen years ago in the town of Huehuetonoc, a remote *Amusgo* village in the state of Guerrero where weaving is a way of life. Her mother is one of the best artisans in town and her father grows rice, beans, and maize. But he doesn't make as much money as he did before.

"Before what?" I ask.

"I don't know," she says scrunching her nose. "He sells rice and we live happy. Then he doesn't sell rice and we are hungry."

The TV is on. Francisca is watching an episode of Tom and Jerry dubbed into Spanish. The mouse and the cat on the screen are more interesting than talking to a, "what is it that you are again?" she asks me without taking her eyes off the TV set. I remind her I'm a writer. I write books about women. She chuckles, not at my answer, which I don't think she heard, but at the explosives that the cat has thrown into the mouse's house. I'm having a power struggle with Tom and Jerry. I ask her if we could turn the TV off. She grabs the remote control and presses the mute button. The letters forming the word BANG appear on the screen. A hairless cat with charred whiskers wobbles away from the mouse's house. Francisca is delighted. "Bad cat," she says wagging her index. Her fingernails are a mess of overgrown cuticles and blood. I think she bites them compulsively; her nails zigzag deep into the flesh of her thin fingers.

Against her father's wishes, Francisca attended elementary school for four years until the day he pulled her out for good. He needed an extra set of hands to toil in the fields with him. A pair of nine year-old hands would do. But Francisca was too young to endure the demands of farm work and became instead her mother's weaving pupil. Huehuetonoc, a hot, humid west Mexican town, was where Francisca learned from her mother not only to create artistic designs for the *huipiles* or blouses, but also to spin a rare type of brown cotton called *coyuche*. Unlike the threads of regular cotton, *coyuche* threads are coarse and uneven. Her little hands grew calloused in a few months, her young back strained from sitting on the ground, legs stretched out supporting the loom on her thighs and shin, head down, eyes focused on intricate patterns. No, Francisca didn't want to spend the rest of her life weaving. She wanted to go places where the words *coyuche* and loom were profanities. Any place was better than Huehuetonoc. She was fifteen, and, as dictated by local tradition, ready to com-

ready to bear children, start a family of her own, cook for a husband, clean a house. Then a boy named Abraham arrived in town. He was a young Casanova who spoke to Francisca about fantastic places that until now, she had only dreamt about: Acapulco, Mexico City, and many great others she could not pronounce because they were in *El Norte*, the sweet north, a grand nation devoid of looms and *coyuche*, where people earned loads of dollars and drove big cars. Abraham and Francisca eloped one sweltering night. He was full of lust, Francisca of desperation.

"Did you love him?" I pry into Francisca's heart.

"Abraham? No, I never love him," Francisca says in broken Spanish as she finally switches the TV off. Carlitos is growing restless. She encircles with both hands his tiny torso—the only place he can be held by—and lifts him up in the air.

"*Qué pasa Carlos Manuel Candelario Herrera*, huh? *Qué pasa niño*? What's going on, baby?"

She throws him up in the air and catches him midflight. The room is filled with Carlitos' laughter. With every one of his belly laughs, he exposes eight uneven baby teeth, four on each jaw. There are no legs kicking in delight or hands outstretched trying to touch his mother's face. But he is happy and his joy catches me off guard. I'm all teared up. Francisca doesn't notice.

"Abraham takes me to Acapulco. There, he has many girlfriends and I cry. I go back to my village but my mother disowns me. I go to my mother-in-law but she is mean and says I'm not good enough for Abraham," Francisca says.

It takes me a while to get used to Francisca's present-tense narrative about the past. Her rudimentary spoken Spanish is devoid of past and future tenses, her vocabulary is limited, and her understanding of Spanish as a whole is basic. I wonder how effectively Francisca and her American lawyer communicate through their interpreter who, I know, doesn't speak Amusgo.

Francisca's relationship with Abraham was choppy from the start, full of infidelities on his part, framed by long separations and silent breakups and relocations. Francisca's worst fear was to be left to grow old in Huehuetonoc, a place where people's futures are mapped out on Mayan brocades. So when Abraham and his brother paid a coyote $1500 each to cross the border into the USA, Francisca became determined to take the leap too.

"I tell him I wait for him a little bit. If I don't see him in four months, don't ever come back for me. I find another man."

Abraham heeded her ultimatum and three months and three weeks after crossing into the USA, he wired his coyote $1600; this time the fees were for picking up Francisca in Huehuetonoc and bringing her to North Carolina where he was working at a tomato farm.

"The coyote brings eighteen men, another woman and me. We walk one week or two."

"How long did it take you to cross the border, one week or two weeks?"

"Yes, one or two weeks. We eat sardines, apples, water and *bimbos*. You know *bimbos*?" I chuckle a bit. I try to explain to Francisca the meaning of the word bimbo in English. She interrupts me halfway through.

"Yes," she says. "Bimbos are like McDonald's but not with the fat bread but with the sliced one."

"Sandwiches?"

"Yes, *sanguish*."

Francisca arrived in North Carolina in April 2003, where she picked tomatoes alongside Abraham for twelve to fourteen hours a day. In December when the harvest was over, they travelled south until they found work. This time in Fort Myers, Florida, and later in Immokalee, where a produce company hired them to pick tomatoes.

"Did you live in the company's camp?"

"*Si*. The name is *Campo Rojo*. There, we live with other four people," Francisca mumbles between nervous fingernail bites. By the time she releases her mangled middle finger from her teeth, the dead skin around her fingernails is gone. A bloody half-moon crowns what's left of her nail. I take a good look at her. Carlitos has fallen asleep on her lap. Her knees are drawn together, her two big toes touching, the balls of her feet apart from each other. She looks like a distracted teenager, like a dreamy Mayan princess waiting for a bolt of lightning, a shooting star, a spell. She looks like she is waiting for something.

"You know *Campo Rojo*?" I shake my head while I take a mental picture of this child mother, just a year older than my own daughter. Francisca has a light complexion, is petite and laughs easily. She constantly hides her head between exaggerated shoulder shrugs and often says "I don't know" when asked a question, as if not knowing were her most natural state. There is a timidity about her that makes you want to protect her. Francisca looks frail and spunky at the same time. She looks lost, then intrigued, then lost again. The world around her is frightening yet so full of unexplored bends.

"In Campo Rojo, each of us pays thirty-five dollars per week. I think it's too much because the house is dirty, hot, and full of bugs and leaks. But what to do? We live there."

Then in April she found out that she was pregnant.

"Were you happy?" I ask.

Francisca shakes her head. No.

"Abraham has many girlfriends and too much drinking on weekends. Sometimes he's drunk for days and I don't see him. See why I can't be happy when I know about the baby? Who is going to be the father of my baby, a drunk?"

They drifted apart emotionally but kept living together. Abraham drank more and Francisca worked harder.

"In case he's not around when the baby is born I work very hard." Francisca's eyes wander off. I would like to know where she is. Maybe in a familiar place that looks like Huehuetonoc but happier, where children don't have to work to survive and where the young man she once loved is still there waiting for her.

"In August I go to Naples to see the doctor for pregnant women and he put his thing on my belly?"

I stop writing. "He put his thing on your belly?" I ask Francisca, looking at her over the frame of my glasses.

She covers her mouth with one hand, then the other, then both. Her belly reverberates with laughter. Carlitos rises and falls on her lap. He makes a limbless wriggle; if he were a normal looking baby, he'd probably be stretching his legs, rubbing his sleepy eyes with his fists, soothing himself with the lullaby of his thumb drawn into the vacuum of his mouth. But he isn't and his rectangular self makes another attempt at wriggling like and octopus without tentacles crawling across the bottom of the sea.

"No, not the thing you're thinking," Francisca says shaking her hands in the air. "The thing that lets you see the baby on the TV. An ultrasomething..."

"Ultrasound?"

"*Si, un ultrasonido.*"

"Did the doctor see anything wrong with the baby?"

"No. He only says the baby is fine. I'm happy." Francisca wraps a lock of hair around one finger, holds it in place for a few seconds, then lets go. "I hate my hair, it's so straight. You know how I can get it to go curly, like yours?"

I suggest rolls and a bit of gel. Francisca is mildly intrigued, but as soon as she realizes that it's as far as my knowledge of hair care goes, she continues with her story.

"Then I'm eight months when I have another ultrasomething and the doctor puts his thing again on my belly." She says it once more, this time, for the effect. I oblige and smile.

"The doctor says it's a boy. That's good news. Abraham doesn't want a girl. A boy is better for everybody. I'm very happy. Maybe a boy makes Abraham a better man. Maybe he stops drinking now that he is going to have a boy."

"Did the doctor tell you anything about the boy's legs and arms?"

"No, he says that the baby has to come out straight away because he's sitting down."

Francisca doesn't remember much of which followed the doctor's words. Just how a wave of heat hit her face; how she felt goose-bumped and dizzy and wanted to be left alone. How the doctor decided for her something about an emergency cesarean, something about an incision across her belly; a terrifying thought. The baby had to be born immediately, with or without Abraham's knowledge, with or without Francisca's consent. She cried in the doctor's office, on the hallway, looking out the hospital windows by the elevator, in her sterile room, on her bed, in and out of a chemically-induced dream. Her head abuzz with questions in the only tongue she was fluent in, a sweet Anuac dialect called Amusgo, questions that had the texture and colors that resembled her mother's old *huipil*. Why is life in America so complicated, the hospitals so big, the people so lonely? What is wrong with the baby?

By the time Franscica woke up, she was no longer pregnant. "The baby doesn't breathe when he comes out and he is in an incubator where all is warm with a light bulb and he is alive," Francisca says.

Her mind lapses for an instant; she crosses her leg forgetting that Carlitos is on her lap and the swing catapults the baby a few inches into the air. I instinctively reach for his underarms they way I'd with any other child but Francisca's expert hands go for his waist.

"He falls a lot," she says rubbing his head although he didn't hit anything.

"How does he fall?"

"Oh, I don't know. Sometimes I forget where I put him and he falls. Just like now," Francisca tells me between noisy kisses that she stamps on Carlitos' face.

After Abraham arrived, a nurse showed at Francisca's bed. "Time to see your baby," she announced. Down the corridor, as Abraham wheeled his wife toward the neonatal pavilion of the hospital, they joked about the baby's skin color. If he was blonde and white, the baby couldn't be Abraham's and Francisca will have a shitload to explain. And if the baby was black, Abraham would know exactly whose nose to punch; the face of a *moyo puto cabrón* who'd hit on Francisca when they worked in Fort Myers. Francisca slapped Abraham's arm over her right shoulder. All they needed was a healthy baby of any color. And in any case, how could the baby be white or black if Francisca had known no man other than Abraham? The baby would have olive skin, wiggly toes and fingers, two ears, two seeing eyes, and a mouth grateful and hungry enough to devour the milk that already pulsated in Francisca's breasts.

What Francisca saw inside the incubator room made her heart mushy and her eyes got wet with tears. Newborn babies wrapped in blankets inside rows of glass boxes. Some of them had their bodies covered by a mesh of wires, hoses and gauze patches.

"Poor babies," Abraham said.

"Poor mothers," Francisca whispered.

They passed tiny, pink babies with emaciated legs that looked like red frogs, the kind of thing Francisca had seen only in Guerrero. The nurse stopped in front of a little glass box. The baby inside it was smaller than the others, even the ones that looked like red frogs. He had translucent tubes sticking in and out of his nostrils and mouth.

"That's your baby," the nurse said to the young couple.

"Can I hold him?" Francisca asked. "I only want to make sure he is complete with toes and fingers and all that."

Cautiously, as if her hands were water and the baby made out of sugar, the nurse lifted his body off the glass box. She cradled him in her left arm, then proceeded to unwrap his body with her free hand. An incomplete baby emerged from the blankets. Francisca gasped in horror. Abraham took a step back. "*Ay Dios mío*," they said in unison, their hands over their chests and mouths.

"Poor baby," he said.

"Poor mother," Francisca whispered, not fully comprehending that the baby unveiled in front of them was their first born.

"Who wants to hold this handsome guy?" the nurse asked in her most cheerful voice.

There was nothing handsome about the little boy. Francisca winced, closed her eyes and turned her head away from him.

"That's not my baby," she said containing her tears. "This is a monster, not a baby," Francisca's eyes moved back and forth between the nurse and Abraham. He agreed. That was a monster not a baby and he demanded to see their son.

By now, they were not alone in the incubator room. A group of people in uniforms was with them. A translator joined in the group. Her Spanish was impeccable, her message loud and painfully clear. That rectangular baby with no arms or legs was their son. Did they want to hold him? No. No. No, they didn't. How could they? He was unbearable to look at, he made them grimace, he inspired them sheer terror.

"For a long time I can't hug him. I can't even look at him. I pray that love for my child comes to me but I feel nothing for months."

"Did anyone explain to you why Carlitos had been born this way?"

"How? Nobody knows. Some people say it's the pesticides in the field, all the white powder I breathe when I'm pregnant. The doctors ask if there are other babies like Carlitos in our families. *Dios mio!* How can they ask such a thing? We have never seen anything like that."

"What do you think?"

"Me?" Francisca tries once more to curl her hair around her index finger. "I don't know. *Yo no se casi nada de nada.*" She knows almost nothing about everything.

Two months after Carlitos was born, he fell sick with a life-threatening pneumonia. He was rushed to a children's hospital in Miami where he battled for his life for over two months.

"That must have been very hard for you, Francisca," I say for lack of better words.

She looks away. My words of sympathy seem to have embarrassed her.

"Do you want to know the truth?" Francisca murmurs, her torso leaning forward as if she were about to tell me a secret. Which she did.

"I tell the doctor, 'Let Carlitos die. It's better. I suffer, he suffers, Abraham drinks. Life is nothing but trouble and sadness since he's born.'"

And the magic that was supposed to bond mother and son slowly became a dream Francisca stopped wishing for. She held him in her arms waiting for love to fall upon them like a supernatural shroud. Instead, Carlitos cried shrieking animal-like wails that pierced her ears, heart and brain. She had numerous sleepless, lonely nights during which she talked to her God in mental Amusgo. She asked for a miracle, for legs one night, for arms the next, for silence, for peace, for love, for death. She got none of it.

"And Abraham?" I ask. "What did he say about his son?"

"Oh, I don't know," she says, shoulders shrugged all the way up at ear level, nose scrunched into a raisin. "Nothing. He says nothing. He only drinks and disappears every weekend. When he comes back from work I tell him I'm tired. He needs to play with Carlitos. But he says that's not something for a man to do. I'm the mother. I have to raise him alone because he's tired from working in the field."

"When did you start loving Carlitos?"

"What do you mean?" Francisca asks me, although I know she understood my question perfectly. She's tired. She's not used to doing much talking. She wants to stop and take a nap now that Carlitos has fallen asleep again.

"When did you start feeling love for your son?"

Francisca says she doesn't understand me. Her Spanish is not that good, she says. She does the nose screwing and the head tilting. I feel that I'm talking to a ten-year-old girl. I give her a yes or no question.

"Do you love Carlitos?"

She sighs and looks at Carlitos propped between us on the couch.

"I don't know. I want him to have at least legs. Or at least arms."

Francisca's eyes tear up a little. In the end, she is only a child herself. At ten she was toiling in the fields of beans of Huehuetonoc, at thirteen she had become a weaver, her loom was her life and there was no *quinceañera* party for her. Just work. She turned sixteen somewhere between Santa Ana, Sonora and Tucson, Arizona. Her feet were swollen after days of following her coyote through the desert, her legs cut and bruised from falls in the dark, her eyes bloodshot from sleepless nights full of nothing but fear. She was still watching cartoons every Sunday morning when she found that that she was pregnant.

"Is that bad?" she asks me in a spontaneous bout of moral qualm.

"You can't give more than what you have," I say, unsure of how to finish my thought. We stare at Carlitos in silence as if looking for inspiration.

"Are you going to ask me about the lawsuit?"

"Not unless you want to talk about it." She seems satisfied with my answer but doesn't say anything. I give it a timid shot.

"I know that your lawyer filed suit against your ex-employer Ag Mart. The suit holds the company liable for medical and hospital costs, lifetime care costs, disability, disfigurement, pain and suffering and mental anguish, among other charges. I also know they are talking about millions of dollars and that Ag Mart is fighting back with everything they can."

Francisca seems surprised that I know so much. "What else do you know?"

"I know your lawyer is very handsome and that he has his office in Coconut Grove." My comment makes Francisca burst in a fit of unstoppable giggles. She places her hands on her cheeks and tells me she doesn't know whether the lawyer is good-looking.

"I don't look," she says blushing.

"Well, I think you should. He's quite a looker." Francisca giggles some more and asks me what else I know.

"I know that the lawyer is trying to prove that Carlitos' deformities are linked to Ag Mart's documented recklessness with pesticides and I know that without the testimonies of the other two mothers—Sostenes and Maria—the relationship is going to be difficult to prove.

84]

Francisca is now looking at me attentively. Most of what I say she is either hearing for the first time or has heard before but it's just beginning to make sense. Her interest gets me carried away.

"I also know that Ag-Mart has sent to authorities the list of the agrichemicals that it spreads in its fields. Do you know that this study of the effect of those chemicals on pregnant women can take years and years?"

Francisca shrugs her shoulders. "I don't know." She bites what's left of one finger nail and asks me how I know all that. I tell her that I read it in the newspaper.

"The newspaper in English?" I nod. "What else have you read in the newspaper about me?"

I tell her that I saw the pictures of her relatives in Huehutonoc the American reporter took on her trip to Mexico. "Did you see the pictures?" I ask her.

"They just come, take pictures, ask questions, and leave. I don't know how they find my family in my village. The pictures are nice? My mom in them?"

It dawns on me that the reporters who wrote about Carlitos never bothered to share the final result with Francisca. The photographer who shot pictures of Carlitos at his birthday party published them in the local newspaper but Francisca never received a copy of them. The reporter who first wrote about Carlitos and subsequently trekked across México until she reached Francisca's little village speaks very basic Spanish. How did she communicate with the Amusgo-speaking relatives?

"*Pos siquiera que no me pregunta nada de la demanda,*" she says. Just as well I didn't ask her anything about the lawsuit. I know more than she does. She doesn't understand why she can't talk about it with anyone, because the truth is, *ella no sabe casi nada de nada,* she knows almost nothing about anything.

Before I leave I ask Francisca one last question.

"What is your dream, Francisca. What would you like to do with your life?"

She wants to study, she tells me, love Carlitos a bit more everyday and live far away from Abraham.

"Don't you love Abraham?" I ask her.

"I never love him. I don't know what's wrong with my heart, but loving? Loving is the hardest thing."

Cristina

It starts with an odorant molecule and tiny pockets of energy, or quanta, lost by electrons. Everything else is vibrational energy, proteins and complex quantum physics. Halfway into the process the receptors in your nose become the key that fits neatly into a detector molecule that acts as a lock. Then you smell. And the journey begins. The sensors in the hippocampus and the amygdala transmute into memory and emotion and by alchemy the smell becomes a recollection. An umbel of trumpet honeysuckles brings you to your knees. It smells like a garden, you'd say, a place that no longer exists, but lives in that single umbel. The other senses oblige; they know the smell is queen, and they close their eyes and cover their ears and the taste buds recoil and all you're left with is the smell. A long inhalation followed by a shudder followed by visions followed by a calculated exhalation. Then you conjure up places, objects, people, breaths, textures and whatever the memory, it's more plentiful and more palpable than you thought possible to evoke.

When I was growing up in Colombia my Mom used to take my four sisters and me to her hometown, Mariquita. This hot and humid little village was a wonderful compendium of all the aromas on earth. The fruit of the mango tree in Mariquita is not called a mango, but a manga, a feminine fruit with a thick, shiny peel that smells like no other mango in the world. Around the corner from my maternal grandparents' house there was a small, dingy bakery. The bread was made with thick, yellow butter and whether it was just out of the oven or cold it had an exquisite fragrance. My granny used to fight clothes moths with balls of naphthalene. In the evening as we all slumbered in mismatched rocking chairs outside the house, the air smelled of all of these. And Mom would take a lungful of this invisible amalgamation, close her eyes and say, it smells like Mariquita, as if the town itself, its people and their cattle were all contained in a single breath.

We breathe to live, but also to remember. Smelling is a wonderful byproduct of being; it's physiological in nature but also profoundly spiritual. You smell with your nose but by the grace of association the smell becomes a memory.

Start small. Take tiny inhalations and quickly release the air so that the smell doesn't get lodged in your soul. If you can see where it comes from, try not to stare. You might end up in the crosshairs of some battle between good and evil. You can look if it's an animal, that's perfectly okay, but why would you? The problem is when the smell is not from a beast but a human being. It messes with your head. It leaves imprints in your memory like you've been branded with a cattle rod. You feel like you want to stick your hand inside your brain and scrape and scrub, scrub and scrape until there are no memories, just a light headache. Nothing smells like death, nothing. That's why once you smell it for the first time, it stays with you forever. Cristina told me that.

I found her living in a junk yard in Immokalee. There were rusted trucks parked on the curb, and beyond this was a line of abandoned bits and pieces on what once must have been green lawn but was now dust, grease, and fuel, and beyond that was a series of aluminum box-like trailers without visible doors. She emerged from one of those, somewhere behind a mound of twisted metal, car parts rotting away in the sun, and a hungry cat that meowed like a lamentation. When she saw me standing by a dry orange tree, she regaled me with her silvery smile and a whip of her black braid over her shoulder. She plunged into a raggedy hammock and I sat under the tree at an old cast iron table covered in dry leaves and dust. She told me her story quickly, in short outbursts of Spanish and sometimes in an unintelligible fusion of Spanish and Zapotec from her native land, San Antonio Ozolotepec in the state of Guerrero, Mexico. She was twenty-eight years old and her life story, she told me, would put anyone to sleep. Boring as hell, she said. Cristina grew up in a small coffee farm, weeding, cleaning maize, and doing odd jobs for other people's farms. At eight she was in charge of the *milpa* and at fifteen she got married to a young peasant with an iron fist that kicked and punched her for three years until Cristina mustered the courage to leave him and move back with her parents. By then she had borne him two children. She lived with her parents for over six years until April 2004, when she and one of her three brothers decided to cross the border with the USA. The coyote guaranteed them a *migra*-free journey for $1600 each. He had found a new passage into *El Norte*--it would be a little bit longer and slightly more treacherous than the known routes, but *migra*-proof.

They walked for seventeen days until they ran out of food and water. On the eighteenth day, Cristina's group ran into a couple of men who had gotten lost in the mountains. They were dehydrated, their eyes bulging out of the sockets, their lips cracked and blistered, their hair tangled up, their speech incoherent. They demanded water. Cristina's group didn't have any. They said no to the thirsty strangers. The deranged men grew belligerent, threw frail fists in the air that punched no one, and collapsed on the gravel where Cristina's group left them to die. They must have been separated from the seven dead people Cristina saw in the mountains.

I stopped taking notes. Cristina shook her head and sobbed quietly. She wiped her tears with the inside of her promotional tee.

"Five women and two men," Cristina told me matter-of-factly. "They were fresh, too. They must have just died just before we found them, because they didn't smell." She swung her legs to one side of the hammock, turned her back on me but continued talking. "They were stiff but fresh. That's worse, you know?" She crossed herself, once, twice. "If they are fresh you don't smell their flesh. It's too soon. Instead you smell death itself."

"What's death smell like?" I asked.

"You don't know?"

I shook my head, no, and resumed taking notes.

"It's a stench, not like blood, not like rotten meat, not like stagnant water, not like anything that comes out of your body. It's just a stink you don't smell with your nose but with your heart," she said. "Horrible, horrible stink." Cristina sobbed some more.

Two days after the treacherous crossing, Cristina was picking tomatoes in Wauchula, Florida, where she shared a thirty-five-dollar-a-week-trailer with five strangers, her brother, and his wife. A month later, the same crew-leader transported Cristina and his other workers to South Carolina where they picked tomatoes for another month before they were taken to Virginia to continue their tomato-picking journey up the East Coast. The stink followed her. She thought the northern states would be good for her because she had heard that the snow erased bad memories. She stayed up north waiting for winter.

"Snow doesn't erase shit," Cristina told me, her face turned a little toward me. "It's a lie. Once you smell death, you're doomed." She swung her legs back into the hammock, looking frazzled, like she had been carrying the weight of those seven bodies for years.

"And men? *Ay Dios Mio!* Men smell like that *cabrón* in Ozolotepec." Cristina looked at me. "Am I crazy?" She grabbed her head with both hands and said, "You shouldn't have come today, *doña*. To make matters worse, I made tortillas today."

It took me a few seconds to muster the courage to ask her what making torti-llas had to do with anything. It was the smell, she told me. Not the taste, but the smell. Tortillas smelled of home, her two children, her mother and her open-fire clay oven. Tortillas smelled of talcum powder and diapers, of breast milk and toys, of the *molcajete* her mother used to grind corn. Tortillas made her home-sick. So *chinga* homesick.

She got up and patted my shoulder. It was best to catch her on another occa-sion. "I'm in death and tortillas right up to my eyeballs today," she said, her hand doing a low salute sign over her nose.

Before we said goodbye I told her about my quest.

"Do you know a woman by the name of Esperanza Vasquez?" I asked.

"Is she dead?" Cristina asked.

"No, she's not," I said.

"In that case, I don't know her."

Rosa

Immigrant farmworker women have to be the loneliest human beings on earth. They go through life the same way they came to this world: alone. They grow without the comfort of a supportive family group, leave their hometowns driven by hunger or fear or both, cross the border with the USA, sometimes alone, sometimes with their children, arrive here looking for other women—the only ones who seem to understand their needs—and in an instant become workers, mothers, lovers and many other roles, for none of which is failure an option. If they are lucky they find a female friend who happens to live nearby, doesn't go up North after the harvest is over, and has a life so well structured that she can afford to be compassionate, available and giving. But what are the chances of that happening in a subculture where everybody scrapes by? More often than not, farmworker women are surrounded by friendships and alliances as transient as themselves. They have unsound love relationships with unreliable men and have lousy or nonexistent sex lives. Their day-to-day is defined in produce terms—the strawberry season, after the beans *pizca,* by the orange grove—and their dreams are the size of the buckets they carry around their waists and shoulders.

Rosa is no exception. I find her in the quaint San Jose Mission: a Catholic planned residential community for low-income farmworker families. Eighty stucco Mexican-style casitas and an array of social services agencies share the grounds in a rural corner of Central Florida called Dover. She is new here. The case workers at the Guadalupe Center, a nonprofit organization relentless in its mission to provide educational, social, and other support programs and resources to the families of Immokalee, found her this picturesque casita that is by all standards a better place than the overcrowded trailer she lived in. Her landlord in Immokalee had sold the trailer park but didn't bother to notify Rosa or her husband Rufino until twenty-four hours before the lot had to be vacant. A few hours before they would have been evicted, Rosa asked the Guadalupe workers for help, and a few hours later, the family was relocated 160 miles away from Immokalee, the only town in Florida that Rosa and Rufino were familiar with. Dover wasn't just any town with an available shelter for the family. Dover was the closest available shelter that the Guadalupe workers could find to the children's hospital in Tampa where a team of cardiologists and pediatricians was entrusted with Camilo's health. It could be said, comparing this house to the substandard tin box where they lived in Immokalee, that they had moved up the ladder, at least structurally. The house is clean, spacious, and has windows that let in natural light.

"This is a wonderful place, Rosa, congratulations," I say when she opens the door. She forces a smile that very eloquently tells me she's not happy.

Rosa is twenty one years-old but looks a lot older. She's got skinny legs, protuberant tummy, generous breasts, and is awkwardly flat around her hips. She drags her feet as she takes short and quick strides that make her breasts and bangs bounce in odd synch. At first, she doesn't make eye contact. She studies me under her long, black bangs. She looks at my shoes, my legs, my hands, my notebook, and stops before she reaches my face. Rosa has dark ample cheeks, broad nose, fleshy lips, and the permanent squint of a woman in constant wonderment. The American life-style never ceases to amaze her. How do gringos manage to live in their crazy country with their crazy laws without going locos themselves?

The house is sparsely furnished. A small analog TV set with a broken antenna sits atop a brown cardboard box with the word ROPA, clothes, handwritten on one side. There are no photographs or ornaments, no center table or mirrors. The house is barren. We sit on the only sofa there is, a rectangular thing with amber foam billowing out of slashed cushions and armrests. If the fabric is not ripped it's imprinted with names and phone numbers. So is the wall by the telephone. Either Rosa or Rufino or both have taken to using the sofa and the walls as their notepads. Baby Camilo is in the same blue car seat he was when I first met him in Immokalee at Carlitos' birthday. He hasn't stopped smiling into space. When he doesn't smile, he lets out hearty outbursts of toothless laughter even when no one is playing with him. I scribble some notes on my notepad. I find his behavior odd.

After we make some small talk, Rosa tells me that she was born in El Carmen, a little town in the Mexican state of Guerrero, where, she says, lives her other half.

"Isn't Rufino here?" I ask.

"Rufino? Yes, he's here, why? Oh, don't you go thinking that Rufino is my other half," she says, her index finger waving a clear No. "I'm talking about my boy. I left him in Guerrero with my parents."

Rufino crossed the border in 2001 when Rosa was pregnant with their first baby. Four years, two DUI arrests, and a near-fatal crash later, he went back to El Carmen to meet his son.

The reunion was cold and laden with suspicion. He looked at Rosa the way a merchant would do at his commodities after a long haul, searching for dents, for signs of use, for reasons to declare his goods damaged. She did the same, although in her heart she knew there was no need to look for traces of other women. There had been many others. Of that, she was sure.

"Men are like that, horny all the time," she says, curling her fingers into a loose fist and moving her hand up and down at navel height.

Who knows where you'd been they thought of each other as they shook hands hello. Rosa was angry, surprised, and happy, all at the same time. Rufino had just emerged from a six-month-long silence that had convinced Rosa he was dead.

"Sometimes he wouldn't call for a week or two. I understood that. But six months?" Rosa raises four fingers a few inches away from her broad face. I scribble on my notepad, *innumerate*.

Rufino had been in jail all this time. He didn't want anyone to know he'd been caught drunk driving. Again.

A week after his homecoming, Rufino was ready to cross the border again. This time Rosa packed along with him. They'd cross together, work together, make money together, be a family. They'd make enough to support their son in Guerrero and would send something extra for her parents. Maybe they could build a restroom with a proper toilet instead of a latrine, or buy windows instead of the mosaic of rags and plywood covering their house's openings.

They paid $1000 each to a coyote who tricked them, robbed them, and abandoned them in the middle of the desert with the rest of the group. A month later, between the money they had earned working fifteen hours a day in Sonora, small savings and large loans, they had enough to pay another coyote. This one took them to California but left them to fend for themselves somewhere on a four-lane highway. Which one? It doesn't matter. A big one. One with terrifyingly fast moving cars in so many different shapes, sizes, and colors that Rosa asked Rufino to sit down for a while so that she could make sense of this hallucinating, fast-forward Californian universe.

Rosa and Rufino arrived at a strawberry farm in February. Those late winter Californian mornings were cold and foggy. They made her feel unusually sluggish and him particularly despondent. He indulged in alcohol when he wasn't working; she indulged in strawberries while working. These white strawberries were exquisite. The white coating so tingly on her tongue that she found herself stuffing her face with them; two in the basket, three in her mouth.

"White strawberries?" I ask.

"First I thought they were white. Then I found out that it was just a powder that covered them. They were pink and juicy underneath the white dust but what I really liked was the powder. So delicious!"

In March, Rosa found out she was pregnant. The first ultrasound came with bad news. The baby she was carrying had a heart problem. It had a hole in it, or at least that's what she understood. It was best to abort, the doctor said, rest, stop working for a while, get stronger, and try another pregnancy some other time.

"Abort? I swear I wanted to punch him in the nose. Who did he think he was to ask me to sin like that?" Rosa shakes her head. "And how could I abort if I was expecting what I wanted the most in my life, a baby girl?"

"Did the doctor tell you it was a girl?"

"No," Rosa says, "But a *sopelote* appeared to me out of the blue twice." This time, she shows me the right amount of fingers. "That's how you know. The doctors never get it right, but the *sopelotes* never lie."

I have never heard the word *sopelote*. She tells me it's a bird, a black ugly looking bird that eats rotten things, loves carcasses and the flesh of dead animals. In her village it is believed than when a pregnant woman spots a *sopelote,* the baby she's carrying is a girl. I tell her the name of the bird in English, vulture, in Colombian Spanish, *gallinazo*, and we spend some time trading Mexicanisms for Colombianisms and before I know we're also swapping profanities and colloquial names for body parts.

"And what's the story with the white strawberries?" I ask to get us back on track.

"I already told you. They weren't white. It was just the chemical *chingada* the rancher sprayed the field with."

"Pesticides?" I ask.

"Don't rush me," Rosa says playfully. "This is my story."

Five months later, Rufino and Rosa packed and left for North Carolina. California was too expensive, too big, too indiscernible. North Carolina, they had heard, was small, friendly, and cheap. Any place was cheaper than California. That's how Rosa announced it to the crew leader. Could he square their accounts and pay them what he owed them? They wanted to move soon to a different place with new people and nobody nagging her about medical checkups or doctors telling her to kill her baby girl.

"Checkups?" The crew leader asked her. "Are you pregnant?" Rosa nodded.

"*Chinga la madre que te parió*...why didn't you tell me?"

"Because that's between my husband and me."

"I don't hire *barrigonas*. Didn't you see all the chemicals we spray here?" The crew leader pointed at the fields with his index finger first and then at Rosa's belly. "Had I known you were pregnant, I would not have given you work, you crazy bitch."

"Pesticides?" I ask again.

"I think so," Rosa says casually. "It's something the ranchers use to keep the strawberries nice."

And it wasn't just the way she had licked off the strawberries like lollipops. There was also this other time when she got accidentally sprayed with pesticides and passed out. Oh, and these couple of weeks when the field reeked of something acidic that burned her nose every time she breathed.

"Those weeks, I vomited a few times a day," Rosa says, making gagging noises.

"What did you do when you found out about the pesticides?"

"*Pos nada*. I just tried to forget what the doctor told me. The doctors here in America make you feel fear all the time. Everything is bad news, everything is complicated. Don't work, don't bend over, don't walk, don't breathe," Rosa says, counting the prohibitions with her fingers.

"Who could bring healthy babies to this world like that with fear in your head?" Rosa does a bad impersonation of a frightened person, shaky hands, white eyes, mouth half-way open.

Camilo laughs yet another raucous gurgle as though he had understood the joke. His ease is almost unsettling. Babies are not usually this passive, this happy, this quiet. I've been here a couple of hours and Camilo looks as pleased and unfretted as he was when I arrived. I ask Rosa if Camilo is always this content.

"*Siiii, siempre.*" Yes, he's always like this.

"That's unusual," I say, but Rosa doesn't understand the meaning of the word 'unusual' and we spend a few minutes on semantics.

In North Carolina, Rosa and Rufino worked side by side in a tomato farm. She had to. The harvest was poor, the rent expensive, the money scarce. The farmer provided them with a trailer which they shared with eight people, each paying twenty-five dollars a week, exactly the same amount Rufino was making at the tomato grove. On good days they picked fifty 25-pound boxes paid at $2.50 each, but on bad days, which by far outnumber the good ones, they had to go home with $2.50 in their pockets, their profit after picking one single box of tomatoes.

This time Rufino made the decision. They'd leave North Carolina for a friendlier, cheaper, more plentiful soil, where he had worked and still had some contacts.

They arrived in Immokalee in August after a long, tortuous road trip in a

1985 car that Rufino had bought for a few hundred dollars. Rosa was seven months pregnant. They moved into the only kind of place available for migrant farmworkers, a trailer park with only one unit left: a rectangular metallic box without windows already inhabited by a family of four.

Social workers in Immokalee are a particularly active breed. They have fine noses trained to sniff troubles in the community, immigrants in need, the weak and the broken, even before they see them. That's how it's done in Immokalee. Sometimes this army of relentless soldiers knock at the immigrants' home to let them know there are medical appointment already set up for them; they show up with food, clothes, blankets, anything. And that was how it was done with Rosa. A pregnant newcomer was spotted, two visits were paid by the social workers, then the third one came with a medical appointment to see an obstetrician in Naples.

"The doctor did an ultrasound. All the while I'm thinking 'please God make the problem go away, please God make my baby girl all good and happy.' When he finished he made that serious face like the doctor in California and called a translator. I began to shake. I knew the problem was still there."

Not only was the cardiac problem of the baby still there, it was worse. How worse? Rosa couldn't tell. All she remembers are the words of the translator, "*Señora, su niño está muy, muy enfermo.*" From then on, Rosa's brain registered fragmented information that included the words "late termination of pregnancy," "still birth," "you might die too," and the realization that she was expecting a boy not a girl. How could that be? She had seen a *sopelote,* not once, but twice.

A month passed by before the next medical checkup. She remembers well that day. It was sunny. The stretch of sky between Immokalee and Naples, where the doctor's office was, was immaculately blue. The firmament was a deep indigo that reminded her of Sunday afternoons in Mexico. She felt nostalgic for the first time since her arrival in the USA. In Guerrero, she used to walk barefoot because it made her feel grounded, like she was one with the earth, and also, she tells me with a slap on her thigh, because she wasn't a shoe person. She felt free in the fields, herding cows, tending to neighbors' goats, feeding the pigs fodder, all of it under a blue sky. A sky almost as beautiful as the one over her head on the 24th of September 2005. She was eight months pregnant.

"The doctor buried his fingers here," Rosa says with her fingernails pointing at one side of her lower abdomen. "I jumped. Of course, the baby was there. I had to jump. I wished I could tell him what a *puto cabrón* he was for hurting me."

In a matter of minutes a medical decision was made. The baby had to be born that day, that's all the nurse managed to tell Rosa in broken Spanish. The world spun fast, too fast for her to comprehend why a stranger had decided on the life she had carried inside herself for eight months. It was a month too early, Rosa didn't want to give birth right there and then, and Rufino didn't know where she was. She had gone to Naples only for a check-up, not to deliver a baby, couldn't the doctor see that? But none of these reasons could rival a medical decision. It looked to Rosa that the doctor spoke more rapidly than the last appointment and in a language more unintelligible than English. It was confusing. The doctor's office turned into a bewildering world where unfamiliar faces, language, and expressions took charge of Rosa's life without her consent. A translator explained to Rosa the concept of a C-section.

"A baby coming to this world through your belly? *Dios mio, Dios mio,* what kind of country is this? That's not how it's supposed to be. They have to be born they way they are made, *si*?" I give Rosa a hurried nod of the head so that she continues with her story.

"You know what else they do in this country?" Rosa asks, the shock still evident in her eyes.

"They give you contractions. *Dios mio, Dios mio.* They give you an injection that makes the baby come faster. That's not good. That's wrong. You're supposed to wait until the baby comes out without medicines or *chingadas.*"

Camilo smiles quietly and stares at Rosa from his car seat. His body is a bit tilted to the left. He looks almost as if he doesn't have enough strength on his left side to support his body straight. I reach into the seat and straighten his body. Almost immediately his giggly body leans back on the left side of the car. From there, he resumes his gurgles of laughter. I look at Rosa, searching for an explanation, but she doesn't say a word. I choose not to press for one.

Rosa didn't have the chance to hold her newborn in her arms. As soon as she delivered him, vaginally as she demanded, the baby was whisked away into the arms of nurses and sterile hospital blankets. Camilo was immediately placed in an incubator. Someone, Rosa doesn't remember who, came into her room to announce that a helicopter was going to fly her son to a children's hospital in Saint Petersburg.

"I swung my legs out of bed. I needed to get dressed to go with my baby. But a white nurse sat me down and told me that I couldn't go. That the helicopter was only for my son, I had to find my own transportation."

The following were the most agonizing hours in Rosa's life. She needed to let Rufino know he was a dad. True, it was a month too early, but the American doctor made him be born. It was complicated to understand, let alone to explain. She went around the hospital looking for Mexican-looking faces so she could ask for a ride back to Immokalee. It was long shot, but she had to ask. How else was she going to make it back home, tell her husband, and find a way to get to Saint Petersburg to see their son?

A Good Samaritan of those who abound in farmworkers communities drove her back to Immokalee. Now she needed to find her husband. Rosa sent a neighbor's son to the tomato field looking for Rufino.

"Tell him it's an emergency. Tell him it's about the baby. Tell him he needs to come home right now."

Rosa stayed in their trailer praying and crying. *Mi niño, mi niño. Dios mio, mi niño.*

By the time Rufino came home, Rosa's eyes were two reddish bulges. She had been frantic yet methodic as she planned their trip to Saint Petersburg. Their suitcase packed, the piggy bank broken into and emptied, the baby clothes donated by the Catholic charities ready to go in a pink bag, the telephone number of a neighbor already written down.

Rufino and Rosa looked at each other, realizing in private silence that they had no way of getting to the hospital without a car. It was a three-hour ride. Who was going to do that for them? Which of their farmworkers friends would gladly drive six hours on a main Florida highway without a car registration, a driver's license, a valid identification card or vehicular insurance? A friend mentioned some nice coach buses he had seen in Naples. They were big, looked clean and comfy, and had a skinny dog drawn of their sides. But how do you get on one of those? Where are they? How do you know when or if they go to Saint Petersburg? Are they expensive? Are they only for Americans or would they take undocumented immigrants too?

"This country is very difficult to understand," Rosa says as she unveils one of her round milk-pulsating breasts. Camilo's lips seal around her exposed brown nipple making rhythmic gulping sounds that lit up Rosa's face.

The friend who had seen the Greyhound buses drove them back to Naples. He wouldn't take them to the hospital. It was a long journey down a highway infested with patrol cars. He couldn't end up in jail, again. They looked around Naples, asked for the buses, went in circles several times, wasting gas, money and precious time until they found the greyhound terminal. The ticket was thirty-five dollars per person. Between Rufino's day earnings, the money from the piggy bank, and another loan from their friend, they managed to get a little over the seventy dollars they needed for the bus fare. It was five a.m. when Rosa and

boarded a bus bound to Saint Petersburg. By the time they reached their
ation and found another good Samaritan to give them a lift from the bus
nal to the hospital, it was five p.m. Rosa hadn't seen her son in twenty-four
hours. Rufino had never seen him.

"You should've seen m*i niño*. Somewhere in the middle of that soup of wires,
hoses and needles, was my boy. I wanted to hold him but those *chinga* doctors
didn't let me. How could I hurt him if he was mine?"

Rosa wipes off her nipple dribbles of milk with her bra. Camilo has fallen
asleep looking at her from the safety of his mother's arms.

"He had something sticking out of his skull. Half of his head was shaved. I
had never seen a bald baby, isn't that a crime? In Mexico nobody would do such
a thing to somebody else's baby without the mother's permission."

"What did they do to the boy?"

"They stuck a needle to one side of his skull."

"Why? Didn't you say his problem was in the heart?"

"Well, let me show you" Rosa says, walking into the next room with Camilo
in her arms. "You know English. Maybe you can tell me."

I walk into her bedroom: another desolate room with no bed. They sleep on
the floor on an assortment of inflatable mats and old sheets.

"It's somewhere here," she says reaching into the dark belly of a half-broken
armoire. A few knickknacks fall on the floor as Rosa shakes and rattles the draw-
ers. Finally, her hands emerge from the armoire with a plastic bag full of papers.
"Here, you tell me what's wrong with m*i niño*. They gave me this when Camilo
was four months old." She hands me Camilo's most recent interdisciplinary as-
sessment from the Children's Hospital in Saint Petersburg.

*His condition consists of a single ventricle with dextrocardia, unbalanced AV
canal with double outlet right ventricle, moderate pulmonary stenosis, proximal
LPA branch stenosis and interrupted IVC. He had malrotation of intestines, vesi-
couretal reflux, polysplenia and a history of seizures and MCA infarct. ...A CT of
the brain showed a large region of decreased attenuation involving the right frontal
and a portion of the parietal globe...*

I read the paper several times but my understanding of the whole medical
picture is basic, sorely basic. The more I read it the more uncertain I am about
its meaning. I don't want to speculate and misinform Rosa. She looks at me anx-
iously as if waiting for enlightenment, but this medical terminology is beyond
my grasp. I can't help Rosa, not today, not until I get help from someone else.

"I'm afraid I don't understand a word, Rosa. Sorry. I can get it translated into
Spanish for you though."

Rosa looks puzzled. I see a sneer under the overgrown bangs that cover one side of her face. I must look like a sham to her. She jokes that I tricked her. That I'm not as smart as I look. "I know he had a hole in his heart and then a piece of blood went to his brain and that's why his left side is weak. Don't worry," she says. "Leave those *chinga* big words for the doctors."

"What do you think is going to happen with Camilo?" I ask Rosa. She squints as if I were the sun shining in her eyes.

"He's going to wake up and I'm going to change his diapers."

"I mean, what kind of life do you think he is going to have?"

"If I listen to the doctor, Camilo won't make it past his fifteenth birthday. But I know he's going to make it. He's a little boy, why would God want to take him away so soon?"

Camilo wakes up and smiles, looking at the ceiling. As Rosa sits him back in the car seat, I notice that his left hand is curled into a permanent tight fist. I reach out and try to unfurl his tiny hand. It doesn't respond.

"What's wrong with Camilo's hand?" I ask.

"The bad one?" Rosa asks and I wonder if she is trying to be funny.

"Yes, Rosa the bad one."

"I don't know," she says with a deep shrug of her shoulders. "He wasn't born like this," she says forcing her finger into his fist. "That happens to all children that have surgery. That's the problem," she says.

"Who told you that?" I ask.

"The doctors," she says. "Well, not the doctors, but the translator."

An awkward silence follows. Camilo coos and giggles and every giggle tilts his body more and more to the left. I straightened him again.

"Are we done?" Rosa asks and her question takes me by surprise. I wonder the same thing. Am I done? Will I ever be?

"Do you know a woman by the name of Esperanza?" I ask.

"Who is she?" Rosa asks. "An actress?"

"She is a farmworker. She lost one baby crossing the desert. Have you heard a story like that?" I ask.

"You hear stuff like that but you turn the other way."

"Why?" I ask.

"Because we all carry our own cross and the last thing you want is to wind up carrying someone else's on top of yours," Rosa says. "Too heavy," she adds and does a wobbly walk of bent knees and uneven shoulders. She laughs hard, then asks me to leave. Rufino will be back in no time at all and he doesn't like her sharing her cross with strangers.

The ABC'S

ALTAR

Undocumented immigrants have several options when they cross into Arizona. The remote Tohono O'odham Indian reservation, the treacherous Barry M. Goldwater Bombing Range, the steep Arivaca mountains, or the traditional path, The Altar Valley, a heavily patrolled swath of desert grassland that extends almost to Tucson, Arizona.

Altar, a little town with unpredictable population located in the Sonoran desert, is a jumping-off place for migrants heading north. They come here to catch a seventy-mile ride to Sasabe, a tiny hamlet right on the borderline, or *la línea*. From there, they make their way into the Promised Land on foot. It's another seventy miles to Tucson.

BEER

Twelve dollars for a thirty-pack. Not bad. Wait until Friday when you get paid and put your beer dollars where your wife can't see them. On Saturday, go to the Western Union and send your earnings back to your country. On your way to the trailer park, stop by the *taquería* or the Dollar Store and get your Key Light and your Natty Ice. Go home, get hammered, get smug, get pumped up, get violent. Throw your kids against the wall if they cry, punch your wife in the nose if she asks you to stop. Wrestle your *compadres* to the ground and roll in the dust. Let it all out. Shout obscenities and squeeze your crotch. Be a beast, feel alive.

COYOTES

9:30 p.m. My house telephone rings.
Hello? I answer.

Are you Adriana Páramo? a Mexican man asks.

Yes. How can I help you?

I have here with me a, umm, Caridad Restrepo. Do you know her?

No, I don't. Who are you, again?

I'm calling from Arizona. She says you've got the money.

I'm not sure what's going on but I don't like the sound of things. I hear commotion in the background and in a fleeting second of self-preservation or cowardice, I hang up.

Two weeks later. It's five p.m. The house phone rings.

Hello?

I need to talk to Mrs. Adriana Páramo, a different Mexican man says.

This is she. Who am I talking to?

I've got your chicken, he says.

You've got my what?

Your *pollo*. Send the money to the following Western Union, ready?

This time around, I'm not frightened. I know that he is a coyote, I know that some of the women I have interviewed and given my telephone number to, are using it as a creditable contact for friends and/or relatives crossing the border. I get cocky stupid and ask, You are the coyote, right? Can I ask you a few questions?

He hangs up.

DEATH

More than three-quarters of border-crossing deaths along the southwest border occur in the Arizona desert. The U.S. Border Patrol implemented the Border Safety Initiative (BSI) in June 1998 with the intention of enforcing border security, educating and informing migrants of the dangers involved in crossing the border illegally, and carrying out search and rescue operations to help migrants in life-threatening situations.

Since 1995, the number of border-crossing deaths increased and by 2005 had more than doubled.

ENTRE EL AMOR Y EL ODIO

I knock on the door of her trailer. I get no answer. I knock again and again. Nothing. The door is unlocked and I let myself in. Rosalba? I call out. The trailer is dark and barren. The last time I was here there was furniture and a refrigerator. I don't know where everything has gone. Rosalba? At the end of the small hall I see the pale blue light of a TV shinning from under the door. Rosalba, it's me, I say as I open her room. She waves me in without looking. She's watching a rerun of *Entre el Amor y el Odio, Between Love and Hatred*, a Mexican soap based on a *radionovela* she listened to back in Mexico. She tells me the TV is new; well, not new, new but new to her. She exchanged it at a yard sale for most of her furniture. She loves the title of the soap, she tells me. That's how she lives, how everyone she knows lives: *Entre el Amor y el Odio*. And how about me? she wants to know. Do I also live between Love and Hatred?

FENCE

In 2006, the Secure Fence Act was passed to build 700 miles of double-reinforced security fencing in areas along the border prone to illegal immigration. This structural as well as virtual fence has cost the US taxpayers over three billion dollars so far, of which millions were spent to tear down and rebuild a section that had been erroneously constructed five feet inside Mexico.

GUMS

Alba's gums bleed when she brushes her teeth. She stops brushing them. Plaque builds up on her teeth, next to the gum, and the bacteria in plaque cause her gums to become inflamed. They get tender and swollen and slowly start to detach from her molars first, then her front teeth. The jaw bone holding her teeth in place is gradually damaged until so much bone has been destroyed that her teeth start to become mobile, loose, and her gums begin to recede.

During one hot Florida summer while harvesting watermelons in the field, she misses a fifty-pounder flung her way. The watermelon crashes onto her face and knocks out a few of her teeth.

By the time I met her, she had developed diabetic neuropathy--a medical condition in which diabetes causes nerve damage in the hands, feet or legs.

She was toothless.

She had just turned twenty-three.

HUMANE

Humane Borders, a non-profit organization founded in June 2000, maintains a network of sixty-five-gallon barrels of drinkable water on routes known to be used by migrants coming north through the American desert. All the barrels are placed on steel stands above the desert floor, are marked by a blue flag atop a flagpole thirty feet high, have *Fronteras Compasivas,* Humane Borders, bumper stickers on them and are painted with the word *Agua* on the side.

Some immigrants think that the barrels are traps. They stay away from the blue flags.

IMMOKALEE

In 2001, The Coalition of Immokalee Workers, CIW, a farmworker organization, launched the Campaign for Fair Food with the first-ever farmworker boycott of a major fast-food company. The national boycott of Taco Bell called on the fast-food giant to, among other things, pay a premium of one penny more per pound for their tomatoes. In March 2005, following a four-year campaign, Taco Bell agreed to meet all of CIW's demands. The Campaign for Fair Food did not stop at Taco Bell. In 2007, McDonald's and the CIW reached a landmark accord that went beyond the standards set in the Taco Bell agreement. In 2008, Burger King, Subway, Whole Foods Market and Bon Appétit Management followed suit.

JAN

In 2010, Arizona Governor Jan Brewer signed the nation's toughest immigration bill into law. Its aim is to identify, prosecute, and deport undocumented immigrants. This law makes the failure to carry immigration documents a crime and gives the police broad powers to detain anyone suspected of being in the country without authorization. It also makes it a state crime — a misdemeanor — to not carry immigration papers or to provide aid or transportation to an undocumented immigrant. In addition, it allows people to sue local government or agencies if they believe federal or state immigration law is not being enforced.

KICKAPOO

The border fence meant to stop the crossing of undocumented migrants into the USA also divides three Native American nations: O'odham, Cocopah and Kickapoo.

The Kickapoo nation resides in the Eagle Pass area of Texas. A span of the fence would go from five miles northwest of Del Río to five miles southeast of Eagle Pass.

In the seventeenth century, the Kickapoo lived in the Michigan area. A century later they were displaced to Missouri, Wisconsin, Kansas and Texas. The Kickapoo, despite living in the United States for centuries, were not recognized as a nation until 1983. Two decades later, various miles of fence will divide the land where they live, and the steel beams will threaten the preservation of their unity, family and customs.

LIGHTS

Think before you flicker the lights five times the way the social worker told you. Think before you let the neighbors know he is beating you again. It's true that he can't punch you if you crawl under a table, but it makes it easy for a kick to reach your face. Think before you creep to that light switch. The lights will alert your friend next door, you were told. What you weren't told was that the trick with the light works only if your neighbor is awake and looking in the direction of your trailer and has a few minutes left in her phone and is willing to call the police who might or might not come to the rescue of a wetback like you. And when the police come, if they do at all, fix your hair, and wash that blood off your face. Tell them that it was all a mistake, that your husband is out and the children are asleep. Remember that a husband in jail makes you the sole breadwinner and how are you going to do that? You'll need to borrow money to bail him out, because, well you need his income. It's best not to flicker the lights. Roll your body into a ball the way you saw your own mother do so many times. Think how lucky your neighbor is. She never flickers the lights.

MONEY

Assume that there are between 1 and 3,000 people attempting to cross the border every day, and that each pays $1,500 for a coyote. That's $500 million in a bad year or a billion dollars in a good one; an untaxed travel industry unto itself.

NUMBERS

8 to 12 million: Undocumented alien population estimated by Homeland Security in 2003.

20 million: Undocumented alien population according to CNN anchor, Lou Dobbs.

46.7 million: Hispanic population in 2008.

65,000: Undocumented students graduating from high school each year.

Between 400,000 and 1 million: Undocumented migrants trying to slip across each year.

100,000: Fathers and mothers of American citizens deported between 1997 and 2007.

4 million: Undocumented entries between 1998 and 2004.

9 million: Apprehensions along the border between 1998 and 2004.

2200: Immigrant deaths during border crossings between 1998 and 2004.

23: Suicides among Border Patrol agents and support staff between 1993 and 2004.

ORACION

Prayer to Santo Toribio Romo Gonzalez, protector of all wetbacks:
For the *raitero*, driver:
I ask the Lord that through the intercession of His Holy Martyr,
I drive carefully and not hurt anyone on my way.
Protect me and those who are with me
from evil and allow us to arrive safe and sound to our destination
In the name of Jesus Christ our Lord.

PICKERS

Jamie Boatwright owns a farm on Chandler Mountain in Alabama. His large variety of tomatoes are ripe and ready to pick, but there's a problem — no pickers. Most of Boatwright's usual workers left Alabama after the new immigration law went into effect in the state. Since then, he's had a total of eleven Americans looking for work as tomato pickers. After Boatwright showed them around and explained the work to them, a total of one of those actually went back the next day. That one worker picked about four boxes of tomatoes before leaving the field and quitting. Boatwright says that picking crops in the fields is a specialized skill that Americans just aren't accustomed to doing.

If Boatwright were to raise his wages in order to attract American pickers, he'd have to also raise the prices of his tomatoes. A price hike would not allow him to compete with the lower prices of tomatoes from neighboring states.

QUIÑONES

Alfredo Quiñones-Hinojosa came to the USA as an undocumented immigrant in 1987. He couldn't afford the going rate for a coyote, US $600, so he crossed alone. He worked as a farmhand in California, earning $3.35 an hour. He learned some English and applied and was accepted to the local community college. He made his way to the University of California, Berkeley and was later accepted to Harvard Medical School. Dr. Quiñones's expertise in treating spinal, brain stem, and brain tumors saves lives. He is also heavily involved in researching the origin of tumors, and in developing new ways of treating brain cancer that might one day lead to find a cure.

ROBERT

In 2011, Alabama Governor Robert Bentley signed a tougher bill than Arizona's into law. Among the provisions of the new law: Public schools will have to confirm students' legal residency status through birth certificates or sworn affidavits. Illegal immigrants are banned from attending state colleges. Transporting, harboring, or renting property to undocumented immigrants will be illegal.

SOUTHWEST

The 1994 Southwest Border Strategy was designed to strengthen enforcement of the immigration laws and to shut down the traditional corridors for the flow of undocumented immigrants along the southwest border. The strategy assumed that by controlling those corridors, the migrant traffic would shift to more remote areas where the Border Patrol would detect and apprehend them. The strategy also assumed that natural barriers such as the Rio Grande in Texas, the mountains east of San Diego, and the desert in Arizona would act as deterrents to illegal entry. What the strategy did not consider was the migrants' resilience and desperation. They kept coming.

Following the implementation of the strategy, there was a decrease in the number of apprehensions and an increase in border-crossing deaths resulting from exposure to either extreme heat or cold.

TORTILLAS

More tortillas than bagels are consumed every year in the United States.

UNBREAKABLE

4:30 a.m.: Wake up. Prepare lunch in your trailer.

5:00 a.m.: Walk to the parking lot or pick-up site to begin looking for work.

6:30 a.m.: With luck, a contractor will choose you to work for him for the day. The job may be ten to one hundred miles away. Board the contractor's converted school bus to go to the fields.

7:30 a.m.: Arrive at fields and begin weeding or simply waiting while the dew evaporates from the tomatoes. You are usually not paid for this time.

9:00 a.m.: Begin picking tomatoes — filling buckets, hoisting them on your shoulder, running them a hundred feet or more to the truck and throwing the bucket up into the truck — all for a token worth, on average, fifty cents. Work fast because you must pick 2.5 tons of tomatoes in order to earn minimum wage today. This may or may not be possible depending on the time of year and quantity of tomatoes on the plants.

12:00 p.m.: Eat lunch as fast as you can, often with your hands soaked in pesticides. Return to work under the smoldering Florida sun.
5:00 p.m. (sometimes much later, depending on the season): Board bus to return to Immokalee.

Between 5:30 and 8:00 p.m.: Arrive in Immokalee and walk home.

The next day, get up and do it all over. You are Unbreakable.

VISA

The H-2A Agricultural Visa Program was passed by congress in 1986. It allows agricultural employers to hire foreign guest workers on temporary work visas to fill seasonal jobs. Since the laborers brought in as guest workers are treated as non-immigrants, they are not permitted to switch employers, can only work for the employer who got them the job and, if they want to come back the following year, must hope that the employer will invite them back.

Of the 2 to 2.5 million farm workers in the United States, approximately fifty-seventy percent are undocumented. These domestic workers do not have the option to achieve legal immigration status under the H-2A program.

The H-2A guest worker program:

- Does not provide adequate protection against the exploitation of guest workers;
- Drives down wages and working conditions for domestic workers;
- Creates an incentive for employers to prefer guest workers over domestic workers;
- Creates an atmosphere in which employers are able to violate the rights of workers in "rampant and systemic" ways;
- Fosters abuse in the recruitment of foreign guest workers; and
- Deprives farm workers of bargaining power and political influence.

WAGES

Florida tomato harvesters are still paid by the piece. The average piece rate today is fifty cents for every thirty-two pounds of tomatoes they pick, a rate that has remained virtually unchanged since 1980. A worker today must pick more than 2.25 tons of tomatoes to earn minimum wage in a typical ten-hour workday — nearly *twice* the amount a worker had to pick to earn minimum wage thirty years ago, when the rate was forty cents per bucket. Most farmworkers today earn less than $12,000 a year.

Farmworkers have neither the right to overtime pay, nor the right to organize and collectively bargain with their employers.

According to the 2008 USDA Profile of Hired farmworkers report, farmworkers remain "among the most economically disadvantaged working groups in the U.S." and "poverty among farmworkers is more than double that of all wage and salary employees."

XENOPHOBIA

Pronunciation: /ˌzen-ə-ˈfō-bē-ə, ˌzēn-/
Function: *n*

Def: fear and hatred of strangers or foreigners or of anything that is strange or foreign.

YEARN

Do mothers' empty arms still yearn for the babies they lost while crossing the border?

ZERO

In the most extreme conditions, farmworkers are held against their will and forced to work for little or no pay, facing conditions that meet the stringent legal standards for prosecution under modern-day slavery statutes. Federal Civil Rights officials have successfully prosecuted seven slavery operations involving over 1,000 workers in Florida's fields since 1997, prompting one federal prosecutor to call Florida "ground zero for modern-day slavery."

Esperanza

I'm back in the same Lakeland neighborhood where, eighteen months ago, I started my search for Esperanza. After a few turns and twists, dead ends, and streets without names, I find a trailer park on Wabash Street where, I was told, a woman by the name of Esperanza Vasquez lives. It is a small village of mismatched prefabricated homes of all sizes and colors that stand one behind the other, shotgun style.

I drive slowly down the dusty, narrow lane that separates the row of mobile homes from a chicken fence that gives the park a cage-like appearance. I look for a friendly face, but the unwelcoming air is all too familiar: doors are closed in a hurry, people peep from behind drawn curtains, children scurry to their hideout spots. As always, I park my car and come out to make myself visible. I walk along the fence until I'm facing the street. A young girl sits on the steps of an off-blue small house at the entrance of the trailer park.

"*Buenas*," I say in my friendliest, most nonthreatening voice. She doesn't say a word but smiles a timid grin.

"Do you live here?" I ask her, pointing at the house behind her.

"Yes," she says. "Why?"

"I'm looking for Esperanza Vasquez," I say. "Am I in the right place?"

She straightens up and runs her fingers through her hair as if making herself more presentable.

"Are you from the hospital?" she asks.

I nod awkwardly. I know that if I say no, that could be the end of our conversation. We examine each other for a few seconds. She must be in her late teens and has a broad face, sparkly brown eyes and plump, pink lips. She looks around and then back at me as if deciding whether or not I should be trusted.

"Wait here," she says, doorknob in hand. The house reverberates when the girl slams the door, and so does my heart upon hearing the girl's voice inside the house.

"*Mamá*, someone's looking for you."

I have just found Esperanza. By now, she has become in my mind a human being of cosmic proportions. She'd be a woman with rough edges and few words, leathery skin, strong arms, and a coarse voice. She'd have a no-nonsense attitude, the stoicism of an ancient soldier, and an Amazon-like disposition. She'd be more courageous than other farmworker women, less innocent, more cynical.

Slowly, the door opens again and the girl comes back out.

"Come, she's in," she says, and holds the door open for me. I squeeze by her. She gives off a tang of soap and cheap perfume as I enter the house.

It is October. A cold front shrouds Central Florida, and the rainy season is in full swing. The air inside the room, stuffy and colder than outside, gives me goose bumps. A petite woman lies on the washed-out couch in one corner of the small and dark living room.

"Esperanza?" I ask her.

"*Si*," she says with a barely audible whisper. I was not expecting to see a dying woman.

"Are you sick?"

"I'm broken," she tells me pointing at her right leg under an old quilt. Except for the leathery skin, she doesn't resemble any of the women I had created in my mind. Esperanza is short, lean, and dark with the kind of patchy suntan that characterizes farmworkers. She looks as though life has been giving her a beating for a long time, and the indignity and the pain of it all is beginning to seep out of her body. Her colorless lips, her disarranged black hair twisted in a pony tail just above the crown of her head, and the two dark bags under her sad eyes say it all.

"What happened?" I ask her.

Esperanza pulls the quilt up to her chin and lets out a soft moan.

"I got run over by a car two days ago." She wipes her tears with both hands.

"I had finished my day *pizcando* tomatoes at a farm in Plant City and on my way home..." She makes a pause and shakes her head. "...that's when it happened. Out of nowhere, *Dios mio,* this car came and before I knew I was under it with a broken fem..." She twists her hand under the quilt looking for the word.

"Femur?" I ask. She nods.

The man behind the wheel, *un viejo gringo*, an American old man, rushed her to the nearest hospital, had her leg put on a cast, paid the bill, drove her home and disappeared. She didn't even get his name.

"Have a seat," she says. I look around for a chair; there are none. The room is cluttered with knickknacks—plastic dolls dressed in hand-crocheted dresses, red paper-mache roses, chipped porcelain vases, an old TV propped between plastic crates, a glow-in-the dark Santa that doesn't glow, a table lamp without a shade.

"Here," she says, patting a space on the couch next to her broken leg. I sit next to Esperanza.

"Is there anything I can do for you?" I ask.

"Yes," she says. "Make time fly."

She waves two bony fingers in the air. "Two days. I haven't worked for two days, and the doctor told me that I had to wait two more weeks before I can go back to the *feel*. What am I going to do?"

I don't have an answer. I don't have a suggestion. I question my own motives for being here. I have been chasing after a story. I found a woman instead. Esperanza falls silent, her eyes fixed on a water stain in the popcorn ceiling.

"I've been looking for you for so long," I say quietly.

"Well, you found me unemployed, cold, and *broken*, but you found me." She pulls from under the quilt a warm hand and cups mine.

She doesn't ask me who I am or what I'm doing in her house holding hands with her. She doesn't examine me, doesn't notice that I'm not Mexican, doesn't comment on my soft fingers against her calloused hands. All the problems of her current life are right there in that spot on the ceiling. While Esperanza stares at it, I tell her who I am, what I'm doing, and why I think her story needs to be told. I tell her that if she wants to talk to me, I'll come back another day when she feels better and that in the meantime I'll do whatever I can to help her.

Esperanza trades the water stain for my face. "Can you talk to my boss and tell him what happened?" she asks, looking at me, through me. Her hand squeezes mine. "Ask him to give me my job back when I can walk again. Tell him that I'll try my best to be there next week."

I ask her the name of the farm where she was working.

She shrugs her shoulders. "Who knows," she says. "One of the big ones in Plant City."

Esperanza, like Griselda, Juana, Maria and other farmworkers I know, doesn't know whom she works for. Since every day is a mad race against each other, the farmworkers go to work wherever they are needed, for however long they are wanted, for whatever the going rate is. They might work one day, one month or a full season in one farm and the next day, month or season in a different one without ever knowing the name of it, or who owns it.

I offer to look her boss's name up in the phone book, but she doesn't know his full name either. "We call him *señor* Eugenio. He is tall, wears cowboy boots and a straw hat," she says. "Do you know him?" she asks. I shake my head.

"Lots of men in Lakeland fit that description," I say. "I need something else."

"He's got to have the foulest mouth in Florida," she says. "I've never heard anyone like that."

"That's not enough, Esperanza," I say. "I need either the man's full name or the name or the address of the farm."

She shakes her head; the corners of her mouth turn downwards. "So, I'm screwed."

"Do you have pay stubs?" I ask.

Esperanza's face lights up. Yes, she does. They are in a flower-patterned cardboard box bursting with important papers. It sits somewhere on the kitchen counter.

As I navigate the dark kitchen, I bang my foot against something metallic on the floor. The sight of a one-burner kerosene stove almost brings me to my knees. I haven't seen one of these since I was a little girl when Mom had to buy one after her landlord shut off our electricity. Instinctively, I look around for more similarities between this house, this particular space, and the houses of my childhood. I find none. Esperanza's house is in complete disarray and filthy. Mom's houses were immaculate.

I don't see any food around the kitchen or a refrigerator. The stove is covered in dust and its electrical outlet is nothing but a maze of dead wires. Strewn on the counter are two dog-eared spiral notebooks, one pair of old Nike shoes, a Dallas Cowboys hat, a broken watch without a strap, a pair of stained socks, a dry lip gloss tube. Amidst all that, I find the cardboard box filled with shreds of Esperanza's life. I look for the pay stubs and in the process I find exorbitant and overdue utility bills, two old eviction notices, a court order, a traffic violation ticket, a plastic bag full of quarters and dimes, and a few bundles of pay stubs. I can't help looking at the weekly amounts paid to her. The largest amount I see in the most recent bundle is for $150. At the bottom of the stub is *señor* Eugenio's signature and a contact number.

"Call him, call him," Esperanza prompts me after I show her his telephone number. "Tell him I that need my job. Tell him that I'll be back as soon as I can."

I dial the number and tell *señor* Eugenio that I'm calling from the hospital to inform him that Esperanza Vasquez, one of his farmworkers, has a broken femur and won't be able to work for a few days. The speakerphone is on. Esperanza hears when he says there is plenty of work and that she can go back whenever she is ready. She smiles.

"Thank you, God," she says crossing herself.

For the first time since I arrived, Esperanza examines me in silence. She takes her time. She taps my wedding ring, looks at my cheap shoes, touches a strand of my hair. The little lie I told her boss has brought us together. A few minutes ago, we were strangers; now we are accomplices.

I decide not to press for information. Not today. It's too soon. Instead, I offer to return tomorrow with some groceries. She nods and smiles.

Twenty-four hours later, I'm back with milk, juice, eggs, and fried chicken. The house is open. Esperanza is alone and in no mood to talk. Her face contorts with pain as she tells me that yesterday after I left, she had to be rushed to the emergency room. A new set of X-rays revealed that the pieces of her broken femur had not been properly aligned when the *white* nurses put her leg in a cast.

"You should have seen the X-ray," she pauses and shakes her head. "One piece of bone on top of the other," Esperanza says. "They were supposed to put one piece next to the other, not to pile them up. I hope the old gringo gets a refund."

Nobody offered her an apology at the hospital, at least not in a language that she could understand. After the X-rays, she was wheeled into a room. Then the lights went off. Either Esperanza passed out from the pain or she was given anesthetics. She doesn't know. When she woke, her leg was in a new cast and the pain had made its way down her toes and up to her shoulder. An hour later she was sent home.

"I made up my mind as soon as I saw the new cast," Esperanza tells me. "This *chinga* leg had to be fixed *a la Mexicana.*"

She called a *huesero,* bone fixer, from Zephyrhills. He came, exchanged a few words with Esperanza, and with a hand saw, he cut the cast. Then he proceeded to massage and realign her bones until both Esperanza and the *huesero* were satisfied.

I cringe but try not to judge.

"How are you feeling today?" I ask.

"Better than yesterday," she says.

"Do you want me to bring a doctor?" I ask.

She shakes her head No and asks me to leave. She is tired and in pain. She wants to be alone before the children return from school.

For a few days I pay her short visits in the early afternoon when I know she is alone. I leave as soon as the soap operas begin on TV. I don't have the energy to compete for her attention against the romantic universe of her Mexican soaps.

Nothing seems more important to Esperanza than the fate of a beautiful maid madly in love with the wealthy man of the house. One day, I stayed to watch a soap rerun with her. During the first commercial break, I tried to talk about love. She was not interested.

"I've watched this before," she said.

"It's the saddest thing." On that episode, the pretty protagonist discovered that the man she loved was her estranged brother. They'd been separated at birth. So tragic!

Esperanza is not the only farmworker I know enthralled with soap operas. A Guatemalan woman in Apopka told me that she had missed several appointments with a lawyer who offered to help her through her asylum process. He could see her only at four p.m., which competed with her favorite soap opera.

It's Tuesday. I stop by to check on Esperanza. She's gone, her daughter tells me. She woke up early, turned the kerosene stove on and cooked from three to six a.m. She left to sell tamales to workers in the field. To bring home fifteen or twenty dollars.

"And her leg?" I ask the young girl.

"She doesn't care about her leg. When I got up this morning she was on crutches wrapping the tamales. She's like that. Like a firecracker!"

It's seven a.m. Esperanza calls me at home. She couldn't find the tomato farm where she was offered work for the day. She drove until her car ran out of gas.

"Are you picking tomatoes on crutches?" I ask.

She answers with a question.

"Do you know who needs a hand today? *Las beeles* don't wait," she says. She sounds desperate. I give Esperanza the names and numbers of a couple of local women contractors, but it's too late in the morning. They're all out in the fields already.

Before lunch time, I'm knocking at her door. This time I bring her a sweater and a blanket to help her cope with the winter months to come. Her daughter opens the door and sits on the couch next to Esperanza. A pair of worn crutches rest against the wall.

"This is my Maura," Esperanza says proudly. "My eldest," she says with words, but her face tells me a longer version: *this is my Maura, my eldest, my confidant, my right hand, my assistant, my translator, my bridge with the American world.*

The girl smiles and reminds Esperanza that today the school is out early. She'll pick up her two younger siblings.

After Maura disappears down the cluttered hall, Esperanza tells me that she had a heart-to-heart conversation with God. "I need to unburden," she says. "I need to let it all out. I think that's what God wants me to do. To get rid of all this poison that's eating me alive."

Today, she wants to tell me everything.

She was born in Puerto de Veracruz, thirty-seven years ago, the youngest of sixteen children—eleven girls and five boys. Born to illiterate and poor parents, Esperanza's fate was sealed at birth. She'd be married on the day of her first bleeding. But she didn't start menstruating soon enough and the family's crushing poverty forced Esperanza's parents to offer her in marriage to a well-to-do Veracruzano, twenty years her senior, before her menarche.

"On my fifteenth birthday, my mother dressed me up in a beautiful white gown made of shiny satin." Esperanza's eyes close lightly. "I thought I was having a *quinceañera* party until the old priest showed up, the music stopped, and my mother told me that my husband-to-be had just arrived."

Three times she ran away from the altar and hid in the mountains. Each time, her brothers brought her back and each time the old priest admonished the whole family for not being able to control a young girl. After the third failed attempt at performing the ceremony, the priest slapped the Bible on the white table, knocking off the chalice full of holy wine, and enraged, he announced that he wouldn't deal with that kind of shit.

"Furthermore," he said, the veins of his temples ready to burst, "*Esta niña ya se chingó la boda,* this girl already fucked up the wedding." The guests gasped in horror. Nobody had ever heard a priest curse. Even Esperanza was shaken by his outburst. The priest told her that her best way of redemption was absolute submission to her parents' will. Esperanza and her suitor were married on April 9, 1984.

For three consecutive days there was music, alcohol, and food, lots of food. More than they had ever seen, more than they could possibly eat, all courtesy of the new husband. During the wee hours of the third celebration day, and after the last guests left, Esperanza's father brought a suitcase packed with her belongings into the living room.

"He said that it was my time to go and be this man's wife. At the sound of the word *wife* I ran with all my might, but two of my brothers tackled me to the ground and brought me screaming and kicking back into the house. Each of my brothers held my arms behind my back while my mother grabbed my face and pinched my cheeks until they were numb with pain. 'It's for your own good. Don't you see? He's a good man. Now go with him if you really love your mama.' And I left with my husband.'"

A year later, Maura was born.

Maura's birth was followed by a succession of break-ups and reconciliations between Esperanza and her husband; each reconciliation ended with a pregnancy and each new birth with a break-up. Esperanza abandoned him several times. She can't remember how many, at least four, she thinks, one each time she was pregnant.

"He never wanted children and I was just a little girl myself. I didn't know how to avoid getting pregnant." Esperanza deepens her voice and stands up ready to impersonate her husband. She wags her right finger in the air as she mimics him. "Your name shouldn't be Esperanza Vasquez, it should be I'mpregnant Vasquez. That's all you know how to say. I'm pregnant, I'm pregnant."

"Was he violent?" I ask her.

"What do you mean violent? You want to know if he hit me?" I nod.

"Mu-cha-cha, he hit me and he hit me hard."

She doesn't just call me muchacha, girl, she calls me mu-cha-cha, with punctuated little lilts.

"Even while you were pregnant?"

Her eyebrows arch way into her tawny forehead. "Ay Mija, all the way until I was ready to pop," she tells me as she draws with outstretched arms an imaginary bulk over her stomach.

After she gave birth to her second child, Gabriel, she left her husband again. She walked west, she remembers, as if looking for the sunset, the newborn strapped to her body with a blanket and Maura tagging behind with tiny strides. Esperanza walked until the sun disappeared in the horizon and Veracruz became a memory several miles back. She and her two children slept under a tree for two nights. By the third day, hungry and desperate, she decided to head back to her husband's house.

Esperanza's facial expressions change in synch with her own intonation. Her eyes, as sad as they are brown, light up when she talks about Maura or little Gabriel. Then, as if by request, the same eyes droop and dim when she talks about the old man who raped her on their wedding night, the man twenty years her senior, the father of her children, her husband.

She got pregnant for the third time. "This one came out eight weeks too early and was nothing but trouble from the get-go," she says. The creature was a baby girl Esperanza named Yohari. She was smaller and bonier than her siblings. Her thin skin allowed a maze of tiny, blue, oxygen-starved veins to be visible. The newborn baby girl required special care: at least one month in an incubator, the midwife told her. Esperanza counted out her savings at the hospital's billing department. She had enough to pay for two weeks only. Twelve days later, Esperanza walked out of the hospital with her sick newborn.

By the time she and her husband had reconciled, broken up, patched up and separated once more, it was 1993; she was pregnant again, this time with little Esperanza.

After the birth of her fourth child, Esperanza's husband brought home a girlfriend named Rosa, also known as *la come hombres*, the man-eater. Esperanza decided to work behind his back buying and selling chickens at a small profit. She would make money, save every penny, then leave. It was a simple plan that worked until her husband found her along a countryside road under a makeshift tent selling chickens. Enraged and humiliated, he threw her chickens into the river, dragged Esperanza by her hair into the car, drove her home, packed two suitcases, and threw the five of them out of his house.

That's when Esperanza decided to take the leap.

"I'd heard good stories about *El Norte*," she says. And north she walked, toward Sonora, close to the border with the USA.

Esperanza arrived in Sonora with one suitcase and four children. She arrived at the closest town to the Mexican border like the other women I have talked to: full of dreams, full of hopes that carried the signature of the riches from *El Norte*. Some women make it to this end of Mexico running away from violent husbands or from the hunger that the free trade agreement has brought to their farms. Some come to Sonora looking for children that their husbands have kidnapped and smuggled into the USA or for a husband or a father they haven't heard from in years. Women who make it this far have a full agenda: work hard, feed the children, save money, keep the family together, cross the border. Live.

Esperanza knew no one, had no money, and wasted no time. As soon as she arrived in Sonora, she walked straight to the church. That's where she had heard coyotes gathered to hunt for potential *pollos*. As soon as she walked around the church grounds, a man sporting a T-shirt with a number 1 stamped on his chest struck up a conversation with Esperanza.

"Want to cross?" The man asked her. She nodded.

"Are all of these yours?" Number One pointed at her children. She nodded again.

"It's going to be expensive," he said.

Coyotes are not fond of crossing children. They cry, they fall sick, they hold the group behind.

"How much?" Esperanza asked.

Number One took a good look at each of the children and then Esperanza.

"$2000 only to take *el brinco,* the leap or jump to the other side of the fence."

"For the five of us?"

"For the five of you."

Esperanza memorized what seemed important: "$2000 for the five of you" and "the other side of the fence." She never bothered to ask what *el brinco* meant. Had she asked, anyone would have told her that Number One did not intend to take them to any place in the USA. Instead, he was about to guide them to the other side of the imaginary line that separates Mexico from the USA in several points along the Sonora border. For that, they would have told her, she did not have to pay. Making it to the other side of the unmarked border was not worth paying for—anyone could go back and forth over the line. The real journey starts at the other side of the line and ends in an American city.

Maura was fifteen, old enough to look after her siblings while Esperanza looked for ways to make money. Eventually, she found a job picking melons in the morning. In the afternoon, she did grapevine thinning or *raleo.* The days were long and the labor exhausting. Nothing seemed to matter. She and her children would make it to the North. She'd get a job, make money, lots of it, then go back home to sunny Veracruz, build a house, send the children to good schools, watch them grow and become better, smarter, and luckier than her.

Four months later she handed Number One the money. She felt the urge to bombard him with questions about the journey: How long is it going to take? Is it safe? Will my children be able to make it? Is it cold? Dark? Are there snakes? But coyotes don't like questions. She knew that much.

"How much water do we need?" was the only question she dared asking.

"Don't go too heavy. A liter each is more than plenty. The walk is short."

The dimming light of a January evening along the border between Arizona and Sonora brought with it a bustle of activity. The *pollos* packed what they could—sardines and salty crackers, water, an image of *La Virgen de Guadalupe,* a picture of their children, wives, mothers, little mementos of the life they were leaving behind. Esperanza was less sentimental. There was nothing to be nostalgic about. She'd lived a miserable life in Mexico and was ready to leave, for good. She filled a plastic container with five liters of water. In a handmade pink bag she packed five cans of tuna and five more of sweet beans, two loaves of white bread, six apples, a bottle of homemade electrolyte solution—a Veracruzana Pedialyte version—and a small plastic bag with salt and wedges of lemon to make more electrolyte solution on the way.

Esperanza, her four children, and sixteen other *pollos*—all men—started the journey across the border at eight p.m. The wind blew angrily across the grassland and everybody was cold. Even the coyote shivered under his cushiony winter jacket.

"Were you in Nogales?" I ask Esperanza.

"Nogales? No, I've never been to Nogales. Why?"

I pull a map of the area out of my backpack. I read the names of possible departure points. Esperanza gives me a blank look. A stare that tells me she doesn't know where she left from, because that's not important, because what she remembers of her crossing is not the names of towns, landmarks, or intersections, not even the name of the coyote.

"You know what happened to me, right?" she asks me.

"I have an idea," I say.

"I'll tell you everything," she says. And for the next hours that's what she does. She tells me everything. With mangled words. With whispers. Woman to woman. Mother to mother. Relentlessly. Breathlessly.

"My Maura carried Yohari, I carried Esperanza, and little Gabriel walked, because he was the man of the house." Esperanza makes a pause and repeats. "Gabriel had to be the man of the house because I didn't have a husband anymore, that's why he walked."

The twenty one pollos and Number One walked all night in silence. Four-year old Esperanza wrapped her arms around her mother's neck and whispered, *"Mami tengo frio,* Mommy, I'm cold." She did this many times throughout the night.

"It must have been the cold, or the darkness, or who knows what, but her eyes," Esperanza pauses. "They were the prettiest thing I'd ever seen," she says and instinctively cradles an imaginary head in her right hand.

The desert wind blew in their faces, harder and colder with each passing hour.

"Little Esperanza's lips began to chap. I spat my own saliva on the tips of my fingers and rubbed it onto her lips to keep them moist." Esperanza stops. She rubs her throat up and down like she is trying not to choke. I open my mouth and try to say something soothing, something appropriate, something extraordinary. Nothing comes out.

"It must have been around four or five in the morning when we finally stopped to rest. I heard Number One comment that the wind had blown some tracks. He wasn't sure if we had crossed the border yet. I sat next to him by some boulders and told him that we were almost out of water."

"And?" he said.

"*Pos,* you told me yesterday that it was going to be a short walk."

"That was yesterday," the coyote said, lowering his hat until Esperanza saw only his chin. He fell asleep against a rock. Esperanza tried to imitate Number One but couldn't. It wasn't the cold, or the sharp edges of the boulders, or the wind, or the thirst what kept her from getting some sleep. It was something else. A pang of horror. A terrifying hunch every time she looked at her youngest.

"*Mu-cha-cha.* That was something else. I felt it here," Esperanza digs her fingers into the cavity between her clavicles, "and here," she moves her fingers to her belly button.

The following day they walked longer hours.

"I caught up with Number One. 'How much longer is it going to take? I think my little one is sick,' I told him, but he didn't say a word.'"

The coyote seemed nervous, uncomfortable, as if the landscape was unfamiliar to him. The *pollos* walked for three nights without asking too many questions, afraid of being abandoned if they complained.

Little Esperanza's body started to cramp up; first one leg, then the other. Her eyes began to sink as though they were retreating inside her body looking for water.

On the fourth night, the coyote gathered the group. He took off his hat, scratched his head, and spat a green wad of phlegm.

"I need to go look for a better route."

"What's wrong with this one?" one of the men asked.

"*Chinga tu madre,* don't you see we're walking in circles?"

"Are we?" Esperanza asked.

"It's not me," the coyote said. "It's this *pinche* wind that's covering the tracks. Wait for me right here, *pollitos.* I'll be back with a better way to get to Arizona."

Number One put back on his hat, dusted some sand off his jeans and walked away from the group. He didn't look back. The group instinctively formed a circle. *Chickens do that,* Esperanza thought. "Whenever in danger, chickens make a circle. Remember I used to run a chickens business? Well, they did that, chickens." Esperanza tells me making two half-circles with her hands.

The sixteen men, Esperanza and her four children waited for another day and another night, their fifth night in the desert. Number One never came back.

Esperanza doesn't remember who made the decision to head back to Mexico or who guided the group from then on. What she remembers is how restless her little girl grew. How she gasped for air, wheezing with each inhalation. How weak and lethargic she became.

"*Mu-cha-cha!* Put yourself in my shoes," she says. "Imagine your baby dying in your arms. Imagine your baby telling you '*Mami*, hug me tight' and not being able to do anything."

Esperanza's face hardens. She tells me that she hasn't talked about this in years; she thought that the pain had gone away, but it hasn't. She tells me that she is still grief-stricken, and tired, so tired, and her despair is pricklier than I ever imagined possible and her pain so fresh and her want so big that they sweep across the room like a dust devil. I can feel the wind lashing my face, tiny orbs of desert sand trapped in my hair. The pain is palpable and pushing its way out of her, bulging through the bags under her weary eyes, ready to burst out of her aorta. Esperanza is about to explode. I'm afraid I won't know how to put her back together if she does.

"When the coyote left us, we had already run out of food and water. We were *jodidos*, screwed." Esperanza sighs then continues. "And you know what my baby did all the while? She wriggled underneath my sweater. She hugged me with arms and legs like an octopus. 'Tighter, *mami*, tighter.'"

They had been walking back to Mexico for two days when little Esperanza's skin turned a hue of blue. She felt cold and dry. Her lower jaw hung in the air exposing a jumble of sticky mucous inside her tiny mouth.

"Mommy I'm so cold," the little girl kept saying with cracked lips caked with dry blood. Esperanza covered her with a pair of jeans one of the men lent her, with her own sweater and wrapped her in a beach towel. Maura fastened the towel on Esperanza's back with a knot, her little sister's body strapped to her mother's.

Esperanza bargained with God, with the *Virgen de Guadalupe*, with *San Toribio Romo*. She asked for water, for food, for warmth. She asked for Mexico to appear in the horizon, for another day, for life. Esperanza cradled her daughter's head with her right hand. Six days without a shower and her little girl's hair smelled like rose water. Esperanza kissed it. It was black, soft, shiny, and it flapped with the wind, like a flag. Esperanza's body ached all over. Every spasm made her feel alive, painfully alive. She felt the blisters in her feet; she visualized all of them as she walked, gathering pouches of pus, breaking the skin, bleeding.

Then she asked God for a merciful death for the five of them.

She kept walking with little Esperanza strapped to her body. Rubbing her tiny back with both hands, massaging her arms, trying to infuse some life into her.

"Give me the longest hug ever, *mami*," the girl whispered.

"I said here in my head, no, no, no, but I knew she was dying. *Ay Virgencita! Mi niña, mi niña*!" Esperanza breaks into a long sob. I stop taking notes and hug her. I cry with her. I bear witness to her suffering and the arc of her loss includes me. Her grief leaves me shaken and it seems to touch everything around us. The crochet-clad dolls sadden, the plastic roses wilt, and the couch, stained and sad, seems to swallow Esperanza whole. She looks so small in my arms.

One more long exhalation and the girl's body went limp. Little Esperanza died with her almond-shaped eyes open, looking straight into her mother's, straight through her mangled body, her dashed dreams.

"Let me carry her, *mamá*, you must be tired," Maura said. Esperanza shook her head.

"No," she mumbled over the wind soughing through the desert. She pulled the towel up to cover little Esperanza's head and kept walking.

"They would have asked me to leave her behind if they knew she was dead. I couldn't leave *mi niña* behind. *Mi niña*, she died looking at me. *Mu-cha-cha!* You don't know what we go through to make it here." Esperanza wipes her tears with open hands.

While the other men and Maura took turns carrying her other two children, Esperanza held the dead body of the little girl under the towel. She doesn't know how long she walked with the dead body strapped to her chest; one day, maybe two. She doesn't remember. They were lost in the desert, walking in circles, hungrily looking in the horizon for a glimpse of anything resembling Mexico, or a border patrol, anything but the barren desert.

"Whenever we stopped to rest, I'd sit away from the group with my little girl. I asked her to forgive me for not having water, for running out of beans, for not having packed warmer clothes. You know, for failing her. So if anyone looked over, they just saw a mother talking to her little girl. But this one time, I got up and my Maura saw her little sister's leg sticking from under the towel. She came *ahi mismito*, right away to cover it and that's when she noticed."

Maura tried to take her little sister away from Esperanza's arms, but they were encircled around her dead body with such fury, with such zeal, that Maura needed help from two of the men to pry open Esperanza's arms. By the time Esperanza surrendered the dead body, her arms had adopted a permanent cradle-like position. The inner edge of her left hand—where little Esperanza had sat—rested on her belly, face up, and her right hand suspended in the air facing Esperanza, cradled an invisible head. She looked demented with her body holding an imaginary child, like a dancer without a partner, Madonna without Jesus.

They stuffed her body in the pink bag that Esperanza and Maura sewn for the trip and one of the men tightened a knot over her head with his own belt. Esperanza knelt on the sand and watched the men dig a shallow hole with bare hands. Someone found a piece of cardboard, someone else slivers of wood. The men lowered the pink bag into the hole and covered it with sand. A cross topped the small mound.

Esperanza hits her forehead with one fist. "I looked around trying to memorize the place so I could go back for her and give her a proper burial, but the desert is all the same. I don't know where I left her, *mi niña*." Esperanza stayed in the same spot for a long time. She tried to cry but couldn't. She was too dehydrated to cry. She knelt by the grave unable to move, her arms still in cradling position, looking at the mound, the cross, thinking that in order to save her other three children she would have to leave her little girl behind. The calf muscles rebelled and turned into a maze of knots, her thighs cramped up, and from her belly button a shooting pain, like lightning, forced a loud moan out of her dry mouth.

"It wasn't me. It was a beast inside me that howled. I screamed, and shouted profanities, and cursed God himself for abandoning us, for taking her so soon." Esperanza's chest heaves, her shoulders rise and fall, rise and fall. I don't know how to console her or what to do with the sea trickling out of her eyes as if she'd always carried it under her dermis, hard like pangea.

"Imagine that, only four years. Just four years." Esperanza wipes her tears with the sleeve of her sweater. She shows me four right fingers. Imagine that, a four-year old immigrant dying in pursuit of her mother's dream.

The group eventually made their way back in Sonora, where Esperanza worked as a cook at "El Pollo Loco" restaurant. For a few weeks she and her three remaining children lived in a shelter for *pollos,* a place where those who wanted to cross the border were allowed to throw pieces of cardboard on the floor and sleep until they squared transactions with their coyotes. At the shelter, Esperanza wasn't the only woman who had tried to cross and failed. There was a Guatemalan woman. She was seven months pregnant two months earlier when she attempted the crossing. After two days of continuous walking she went into labor. She squatted under a cactus tree to give birth to a little creature covered in blood and a white paste. The baby was stillborn. She named him Jesus.

"Imagine that. A dead baby Jesus," Esperanza says then she continues with her story. She met a different coyote who was about to take a group of men across.

"How many are you?" The man asked her.

Esperanza pulled her hand out of her sweater and showed him five fingers. Then she remembered; she folded her thumb over the palm of her hand and showed him again.

"Four, huh? All the way or *el mero brinco,* just the jump?"

Esperanza kicked her shoes to one side and let the man see her blistered feet. He understood. She had already tried to make it but failed. He knew the signs; everybody in Sonora did.

"Forty dollars apiece but for *el mero brinco.*" Esperanza strained her ears and asked the man to repeat his price. "Forty dollars apiece but for *el mero brinco,*" he repeated. It was impossible. Esperanza had just paid $2000 to a man who had also promised to help her take the leap.

"You know a coyote that goes by Number One?" Esperanza asked.

"No. Are you sure he is a *pollero*? I know them all and I don't know any Number One."

Esperanza never asked Number One what *el brinco* was. She assumed that for $2000, he'd deliver them somewhere in America called Arizona, a place where Mexicans get well-paid jobs in every corner.

"If I was going to make it to the other side, I couldn't go around moping and whining about my bad luck. Number One screwed me out of my money. So? What was there for a woman like me to do? Go back? No. To what? To that *cabrón* in Veracruz and his Rosa the man-eater?" Esperanza rolls her eyes and smiles. "My only way was forward, towards the North."

She straightens her dress and tells me that as soon as she and her children started their second trip to *El Norte,* she thought that Maura was going to die. The girl hadn't recovered from the previous trek. Maura was weak and feverish, and since her sister's death she'd been hallucinating and behaving erratically.

This time the coyote led her, her children and a group of men across the steep hills that separate Sonora from Arizona.

"Arivaca?" I ask.

"Ari what?"

"You walked across the Arivaca mountains?"

"How would I know?" she says. They were high, steep, and treacherous; that's all she knows.

By the end of the second day, Maura fell gravely sick. Her feverish mind was filled with images of her little sister and *sones jarochos* from her beloved Veracruz.

She held conversations with her dead sister, laughed and cried while staring into space. Then came the vomit. She threw up projectile-like streams of a green and yellow viscous matter. Then severe diarrhea hit Maura's empty stomach.

The other migrants, worried that Maura might die, gave her cigarettes.

"They said that the smoke would make her feel less hungry and stronger." An incredulous grin lands on one corner of Esperanza's mouth.

"Imagine that. Cigarettes. Where have you heard such *chingada. Mu-cha-cha*!" Maura's vomiting and diarrhea were followed by a dry cough, each fit of which turned her face purple as she gasped for air. In a desperate attempt to keep her daughter hydrated and alive, Esperanza decided to extract the juice of the *biznaga*. The Devil's Tongue Barrel Cactus.

"I found a gigantic one. Much bigger than the biggest pineapple I'd ever seen and *todititica* covered with needles as sharp as a butcher's knife. I took away the thorns one by one. I got needles stuck here and here and here," Esperanza takes my hand and places it over invisible marks on the inside of her brown arms, her wrists and the tips of her fingers.

"The coyote told me to stop. I was going to *chingar* my hands for life, but I didn't care. I kept dethorning the *biznaga* until I cracked it open. I squeezed the juice into Maura's mouth. *Mu-cha-cha,* my Maura's lips were *todititicos* white and chapped."

As Esperanza forced Maura's mouth open to squeeze the juices of the *biznaga* inside it, she noticed that Maura's skin had lost elasticity; when touched, it sagged into a fold.

"Did the *biznaga* help?" I ask her.

"Noooo, *mu-cha-cha*. That damn *biznaga*! I thought the juice was going to help her but it almost killed her. It only made her diarrhea worse."

As the group approached a pre-arranged pick-up point, the coyote grew increasingly paranoid about *la migra*. Maura was so sick and Esperanza so drained and blistered that the coyote asked her to show herself on the road so that the border patrol would pick them up and return them to Mexico. She and Maura were being a liability to him, he explained. Esperanza refused to give herself up and pushed on until they finally made it to a place she knows only as "*Las Marranas.*" It must have been close to Phoenix, Esperanza thinks, because from the small room where the twenty of them were housed, she could spot city lights at night.

The housekeeper at "*Las Marranas,*" an old man nicknamed "El pájaro," recognized Mauras's symptoms as those of typhoid. He had seen hundreds of cases, he told Esperanza; all of which he claimed to have cured with a great American medicine called Pepto-Bismol.

"And sure enough, in a week my Maura was good as new."

"A week?" I ask her. "How long did you stay at *Las Marranas*?"

"Twenty days and nineteen nights."

I look at Esperanza as if giving her time to reorganize her recollection.

"Twenty days and nineteen nights," she repeats. While at *Las Marranas*, the coyote informed his group that getting them to their final destinations was going to cost them $1500 each.

"That's why we took so long there. Where were we going to get all that money? We didn't even know where we were. They all called relatives and friends here in America, you know, asking for money. But *mu-cha-cha*, $1500 is a fortune. It takes more than one phone call and more than one cousin or one friend to get it."

"How about you? Did you know anyone in the USA?"

No, she didn't. Esperanza tells me that she made a deal with the coyote. He would send her to Florida to work for a man who would ensure Esperanza paid back the $6000 she owed him. Esperanza and her three children were sold.

"How much did you agree to pay each month?" I ask her.

She shrugs her shoulders and gives me one of her blank stares.

"The man had just brought me and my children across the desert. Don't you see? I owed him big time. He said I was ready to go to work. That was all I wanted to hear."

After two days on the road and several stops in New Mexico—where they were left hidden in a ditch overnight because of an engine problem—Tennessee, and somewhere else that Esperanza doesn't remember, there remained only five of the initial twenty immigrants. The other fifteen had been distributed in different farms along the way.

On April 10 2001, before sunrise, Esperanza and her three children arrived in Lake Placid. The man waiting for them was a short and stout crew leader named Salvador.

"Ready to work, *pollitos?* Those were the first words out of the new boss's mouth. Salvador rubbed his hands together as he examined his new workers. They must have looked pitiful. They had walked for four days, nearly starved for twenty at *Las Marranas*, had been on the road for three. They were dirty, hungry, weary. The only thing in their minds was food and some sleep.

Salvador moved his oblique eyes back and forth between Maura and Esperanza.

"I'm telling you this for your own good so you know. In America, education for Mexican children is useless. Ok? It's a waste of time. So you'd better bring them to the field with you and teach them to work. At least bring this one," he says pointing at Maura, "this one is ready to work."

"Was Salvador the owner of the farm?" I ask Esperanza. She laughs and in between laughs she tells me that she has never met a Mexican farmer in the USA. Salvador was just a middle man. One of those Mexicans that provide American farmers with cheap labor.

"The farmers are all *bolillos,* white people. We never see them and they never see us. Well, some of them have huge houses next to the farm with circular driveways and the whole *chingada,* but they never talk to us."

Salvador took the group to a small house flanking the orange groves. There were two families already living in the house and Esperanza and her children had to sleep on the floor of the living room. It didn't matter. They were in America. A-me-ri-ca. Outside the house, two rows of trailers stood one in front of the other. Esperanza wondered why the trailers were locked from the outside. Maybe there were thieves in the area. She didn't know that the farmworkers living in the trailers were Salvador's prisoners; they all owed him money, they were his property.

The following day, the *chivero* came to pick her up at four a.m.; thirty minutes later, Esperanza was climbing a twenty-foot ladder with an empty canvas bag slung across her chest. She was high up at the top of an orange tree. She didn't like heights and the ladder moved in and out of the treetop with her own weight, like the buoys off the Veracruz shore. She filled the bag with twenty kilos of oranges and as she climbed down the new blisters in her feet popped; she felt squirts of warm liquid run down the soles of her feet. It was a difficult and dangerous job. Esperanza climbed up and down several times, moving the ladder around the tree until it had no oranges left. She must have looked like a ballerina dancing a perilous suite at the top of her first orange tree. And the second, and the third, and the many more she worked on for two years without receiving a penny.

"Salvador told me that I had to work two years in Florida to pay off my debt to the coyote, but then he changed his mind. He told me I had to go to one of the Carolinas to pick more oranges. What was I going to do? A debt is a debt, so to Carolina I went."

For two years, whether in Florida or in Carolina, Esperanza worked seven days a week. On Sundays Salvador gave his workers two hours to do the washing and buy food from his own mother's convenience store.

"Nice little business to have, don't you think? He worked us to exhaustion, didn't pay us, and when we were hungry we had to buy the food from his mother."

"How did you buy food if you didn't have any money?" I ask her.

"On credit."

"Credit?

"Yes, credit. After I finished paying my debt, I had to work some more to pay what I owed Salvador's mother for food."

There are no traces of anger in her voice. She is matter-of-fact.

"That's when I decided to leave Lake Placid. *Mu-cha-cha!* It wasn't easy but I left."

Esperanza had paid off her debts when she told Salvador in front of everybody that she and her children were leaving. He threatened with smashing their heads with a baseball bat if they left.

"If you're going to beat the four of us up, you're going to make one hell of a mess," Esperanza told Salvador as she and Maura walked away; she held Yohari's hand, and Maura and Gabriel followed behind. They walked to the main road and hitchhiked to a nearby town.

"Which town?" I ask.

"I don't know. We went from town to town."

In 2003 Esperanza went to live in Dover, a small strawberry community in Central Florida. Soon, Esperanza found not only work in the fields picking strawberries but a magical yellow concoction that had the power of conjuring up little Esperanza's face. She found beer. Esperanza drank, sometimes to remember her four years with little Esperanza, *su niña*, and sometimes to forget her loss.

"I'd be *pizcando* strawberries and I'd hear her voice. "Mommy, hold me tight," or "Mommy, I'm cold," and I would go around the field looking for her over the shrubs and under the trees. I saw and heard *mi niña* everywhere, even in my sleep. The other women in the *feel* told me that I was going crazy in the head."

Two years of deprivation, living under Salvador's watchful eyes, had not given Esperanza time to mourn her little girl's death. Now working six days a week in Dover, away from Salvador's prison and with her children attending school, she had time to mourn. Esperanza bought a barely functional secondhand car and lived on the edge of insanity for a long time. She worked hard, drank hard, and drove hard—so hard that she barely remembers the day a police officer pulled her over and took her to jail for driving while intoxicated.

"Those were the most expensive beers of my life." Esperanza smiles, winks, and taps my hand, all at the same time. "It cost me one month in jail, $500 for the bail, $1200 to get the car out of impound, and one year of probation, whatever that means."

"Are you still drinking?"

"*Mu-cha-cha!* Have you been listening? Those few beers cost me as much as coyotes charge to bring one person to America. No, no way. I didn't touch that *chingada* again."

From Dover, Esperanza moved to Plant City, and from there to Lakeland. She came to live in a trailer on Hamilton Road, just a short drive away from my own house.

"Have you been to Hamilton Road?" she asks me.

"Yes, I went there looking for you."

"That's some place, that Hamilton Road," Esperanza says. "I paid $125 a week but had to leave after two years because the trailer was too old. It was all right for a while, but then it started to fall apart."

A hurricane blew away one part of the roof that the American landlord never cared to repair. With the hurricane came the rain; during that summer Esperanza and her children ran from room to room fleeing the rivulets of water pouring into their trailer.

Then Esperanza moved to Gallatin Street, into the condemned trailer that the American landlord rented out for $600 a month. Four months later, she and her children sneaked out of the trailer and moved to Wabash Road, where I found her.

"Do you like it here?"

"It's a roof over our heads," she answers, resorting to a quirk I have learned to expect from farmworkers—they speak in plural when they don't want to talk about personal preferences. "For $140 a week we get a whole house to ourselves. The children have only to cross the street to go to school, plus the farms are nearby and most of the time I don't have to drive too far to find *chamba,* work."

She asks me to go in the kitchen and bring the box with important papers. She wants to show me *las beeles,* so that I can have a better idea of her financial responsibility.

"So you understand why I couldn't lay on the couch to nurse my fracture for two months," she shouts from her room. "Imagine that, lying on the sofa with my leg sticking up in the air like a rich woman. *Mu-cha-cha!*" I hear her scoff and think to myself that her body and soul must be made out of some indestructible matter; of something unbendable, unbreakable, unassailable, or at least, I think, quick, self-reparable.

We go through her monthly bills together. I write a list of monthly expenses on a piece of paper so Esperanza can correct me if I'm wrong.

$560 for rent + $250 for utilities + $300 for car payments + $50 for telephone = $1160

I tell Esperanza that I don't understand how her present life can be better than life back in Veracruz.

"Say I get this Friday $140 for a week's work. It would take me several months in Mexico to make that money."

"What's the point of making $140 a week if your weekly expenses are more than what you make?" I try to reason.

"My children are bilingual, I have a house to myself, I drive my own car. See how it works?" Esperanza makes a pause and exhales a long sigh. "I don't fool myself. None of us do. We can't dream certain things because we are undocumented. There are things we can't have because we're wetbacks, but still, where would this country be without us? You tell me. Which *bolillo* would pick tomatoes for two dollars an hour as I have done, huh?" We look at each other in silence. We know the answer. Without the undocumented immigrants, the USA would be a much less productive nation with higher inflation and the difficulty of finding cheap, reliable labor.

"My dream is simple: to see my children become someone in life. Not a wanderer like me. Not a loser like their mother. See? My Maura already finished high school and my other two are ready to graduate." Her face brightens up as she says *my Maura*.

Yet none of her children will ever be able to attend college in the USA, not for as long as they are undocumented. Not for as long as they are members of this legion of eleven, fifteen, twenty million undocumented immigrants in the USA forced to sell their manual labor under the table and for unjust salaries. The girls will soon become pregnant, will grow to be some white woman's maids, or farmworkers' wives, girlfriends, lovers; and Gabriel will become a farmworker himself, maybe a construction worker, or join a gang, or go around impregnating girls who, like Maura and Yohari, have nowhere else to go but a man's bed.

Only an amnesty can change their fate. Only an immigration pardon that gives them legal presence in this country can turn them into nurses, engineers, social workers, anything they choose.

"Is that what you think?" Esperanza asks me. Her eyes wide open, her expression solemn.

"*Sí señora.*"

"If that's true, you should run for president of the United States." Esperanza stands up and places her right hand over her heart the way she's seen American people do when they hear the national anthem.

"I can't." I say. "I wasn't born in this country."

"Are you messing with me?" Esperanza asks, a mocking grin across her face.

"*No señora*. I'm an immigrant too." I also begin to smile.

"Like me?"

"Basically."

"*Mu-cha-cha,* we're all screwed for real."

"I guess," I say while I feast my eyes and ears on Esperanza's earthy laughter. She looks beautiful and alive as she laughs with a mouthful of white, perfectly straight teeth. Her hair, up in a pony tail, gives Esperanza a child-like look, but her arms, muscular and sunburned, are the arms of an old farmworker. She is both and neither. I think Esperanza is a non-existent third woman trapped halfway between the two.

Dreams

While I was looking for Esperanza, I encountered many other undocumented women. I asked them about their dreams. What I heard was a collective song, a kind of wild a cappella chant. Their hopes mirrored each other and in that sameness I forgot whose dream belonged to whom. I let the litanies become images and the images fused into one another until they created a continuum. I got lost in the flow.

I pray that my children remember me; I ask God they don't forget that I left Mexico for their own good, so they could have a better life. Children forget how to love their parents if they're not together. But I call them and remind them that better apart and full than together and starving, *si o no*?

Who, me? Oh, I don't know. A good car, like a second hand Corolla, a computer for the kids and a fan for these damn summers. I've seen these fans on TV. They are towers like this tall and very quiet. How do they work, you know?

I dream of a house up in the mountains where I grew up. Fine looking, with proper plumbing, an indoors bathroom and running water; like the rich, you understand?

You ask the funniest questions. Ummm, my dream? To have papers, maybe an American passport. Wherever you go, people see your blue American passport and they treat you nice.

That this worthless *puto cabrón* husband of mine stops drinking.

To go to school. I always wanted to be a nurse. They look so important in those white uniforms. Can you imagine me with that *chingada* they carry around their necks, listening to people's hearts and shit? I used to be very good with animals back in Mexico. I know it's not the same, but still.

I'd like to own my own place. I've been evicted twice. They throw all your things in the yard. They don't ask. They don't say a word, those eviction people. They march in and throw everything out of your house.

That my children go to college. They can't go now because we're wetbacks. After they finish high school they'll come to the fields like everybody else. It makes you wonder, what's the point, right?

Listen to my dilemma: I don't have papers, therefore, I don't have a Social Security number, therefore, I can't register or insure a car, therefore nobody gives me a driver's license, therefore I drive without registration, proof of insurance or driver's license, therefore every time the police pull me over, I end up in jail. Six times so far, therefore, six court appearances, six bails, six wads of money to take the car out of the impound lot. So, the answer to your question is: a driver's license. That'd be nice.

That this *perro chingalamala* treats me good like those *papi chulos* in the soap operas. I close my eyes and dream of a different man, one that looks like Pedro Infante riding a white horse, with a big ass sombrero and a smile full of pearly teeth. I come out on a balcony and there he is with a mariachi band singing *rancheras*, just for me. And I'm loved. I'm special.

Teeth. I look disgusting without teeth. This white doctor offered to make a set of dentures for me. For free. He brought cameras and newspaper people and we shook hands in front of everyone. He called this "*pro-bono*" or something like that. But I've gone several times and he never gives me the teeth he promised. The other day, his assistant gave me an unclaimed set of false teeth but they hurt my gums because they were made for somebody else's mouth. I'm only twenty-three. I dream of teeth.

Home. Veracruz without hunger. Fat chickens roaming freely in my parents' farm.

This is for real. One day I dreamt that I had gone to the supermarket and bought lots and lots of food. I had money to pay for all of it. When I came out, my *niños* couldn't believe their eyes when they saw all those shopping carts full of toys and food. We ate fried chicken on our way home. Then I woke up.

Make lots of money and go back to Mexico. Buy back the land we lost. Grow maize again.

That my boy grows limbs. I know that's not going to happen, but that's my dream. If not full limbs, at least little stumps, anything, so the doctors can give him the prostheses that he needs.

To see the *cabrones* who did this to me in jail. To drug them the way they drugged me and stuff every orifice in their bodies with raw meat like they did to me.

Do you really want to know what I dream? I dream that people respect me. That the other parents in my children's school don't look down on me because I don't speak English; that they invite my kids to their houses to play.

I want to be able to go to work without having to look over my shoulder. I don't want to be afraid. Living and working in fear messes with your head. You start to think that you're a criminal.

If I could have it my way, I'd get my child back from the DCF. I've been sober for a long time and have a job. What else do I need to do to get her back?

I've never seen the ocean, only in pictures. It's like a wide river that never ends. Blue and calm. That's what I want. I know the ocean is somewhere nearby. Maybe one day when I have papers I'll ask which way the sea is and drive my kids there. We'll play in the water then drink 7-Ups on the beach.

Sometimes I look at my son and imagine that he doesn't have a cleft palate. His mouth is whole and he's beautiful.

Sometimes I look at my son's chest and imagine what his life is going to be like with a sick heart.

Sometimes I look at my baby and wonder if his left side will ever be as healthy as his right.

Sometimes I look at my son and pray he doesn't need a liver transplant like his little brother. He died.

It depends. I have a dream for tomorrow: That it's not as cold as it was today and that my car starts and that I can make it to the field on time. For next the year: To be out of here. Back in Guerrero with my family.

That the money I send home is enough so my children never have to come to this country. That's my dream.

My dream is to be a famous weaver and have my own factory where we weave stuff for tourists all over the world. But not here, of course. Back at home with my people.

To forget everything from the moment I crossed the line right up to today.

I dream of silly things. My own shit instead of hand-me-downs, money to pay the *beeles,* and a one-way ticket back to Mexico. That's all I want.

I pray that my three girls find good husbands, that they don't get pregnant, that they don't end up in a gang.

When I was all messed up in the head, I used to dream that I was an eagle and that I could see where my little daughter was buried and that I whisked her up in the air and took her back to Veracruz to give her a proper burial. But my head is clear now. I don't dream that anymore. I know I'll never find her.

Epilogue
On Writing And Grief

Five months after I found Esperanza, my mother died. Her death coincided with the final stages of my research. I was spending most of my time classifying information, tidying things up, deciding whose interviews were still pending, needed to be repeated or corroborated and which areas I had left unexplored and were in need of further investigation. I was near the end of the research when my mother died, in Colombia. And although Esperanza had been the focus of my life over the previous two years, I didn't think about her at Mom's funeral or at her cremation or when we placed her ashes in the little wall sarcophagus inside a church in my sisters' neighborhood. I didn't think about any of the women I had interviewed. Suddenly, their tragedy seemed alien to me. I had flown home, to Colombia, to bury my mother, and nothing of what had happened in the past seemed important anymore. None of that was real. My mother is dead, I repeated in my head. My Mother is Dead. That was real.

When I was eleven, my four older sisters, Mom and I took our first trip to Arboletes, a small town on the Atlantic coast. As soon as we got off the derelict bus I held Mom's hand and pushed forth. I wanted us to be the first to see the ocean. She held my hand steady and said, No, we're a family, we see the ocean together. And together we marched across unknown streets, hauling our belongings in cardboard boxes. We climbed a steep hill, then another, and as we crossed the street Mom looked down to the right and pointed at something below. The ocean welcomed us with whimsical hues of blue and liquid strokes of undulating aquamarine. Awestruck, we stood in the middle of the street until some traffic light changed to green and the drivers honked their horns at us, called us damn tourists and asked if we had never seen the damn ocean.

"No, we haven't. Thanks for asking," Mom said and we laughed.

The following day we went to the mud volcano, a hot-spring-like pool of bubbling slurry which Mom assured us would cure all her pains and aches. We put on our bikinis and jumped into the muck. The grey pool of mud pushed us upwards to safety and we smelled the gas and the prehistoric deposits lying underground. We gave each other massages, Mom gave me a face mask and I rubbed medicinal sludge onto her sore lower back muscles. We dipped our hair into the muck, made funny faces, stuck out our tongues and one of my sisters rolled her eyelids up, exposing the white bits of her eye and bared her teeth. She looked terrifying and funny at the same time. Terror and laughter made me pee a little in the mud.

Mom, the eternal worrier, was unusually relaxed and carefree. She said that since we were the only ones in the volcano, we could do whatever we wanted. The next minute, we were naked. Mom shook her head as she leaned against the crater walls with our bikinis in her hands. We five girls wobbled to the center of the crater, asked Mom to turn around, and when we told her to look again, we mooned her; asses shaking up in the air, our faces buried in the muck, holding our breath and withholding fits of hysterical laughter that escaped and bubbled all the way to the surface. And this, almost thirty years later, was all I could think of as my mother lay in her casket. My four sisters and Mom, their laughter, our bodies covered in organic sludge, our first trip to the ocean, together, the five of us and Mom. Those were the only women I thought of as we laid Mom to rest.

I hit a wall after my mother died. I returned to my home in Florida and tried in vain to finalize my research with undocumented women. I discovered a string of unsuspected losses: hope, confidence, purpose. Continuing my research, focusing on other women seemed an act of betrayal, a disloyal negation of her death, an insult to the memory of the bravest woman I'd known: a single mother of six after my Dad walked out on us when I was seven. I would sit in front of my laptop, heaps of hand written interviews on each side of it, cups of half drunk Colombian coffee on my desk and window sills, our dogs lying somewhere at my feet. I waited for the nagging feeling to finish the project. Instead, I would get sucked into a cosmos of trivialities. I listened to the kitchen faucet; it had been leaking for weeks. I wrote down on a post-it: Plumber's tape for kitchen. One of our dogs developed a rash on her tummy. She licked and scratched uncontrollably. Another post-it: Get Hot Spot for Honey. I turned the computer off. Saw my reflection in the black screen and noticed two forming folds on each side of my nose running down to the corners of my mouth. I turned the computer back on and Googled, Is Botox safe? One day, I opened the manuscript and searched for the word Esperanza. It appeared 263 times. I have never liked odd numbers. I went to the last line and wrote Esperanza, once more. There. That's better. 264 times. I felt accomplished. I treated myself to a tall glass of Riesling. Went back to the laptop and I stayed with my fingers hovering above the keyboard until it was obvious that I would not write a single word. I turned the TV on, tuned in to the Cartoon Channel and watched two and a half hours of *The Roadrunner*. And I laughed. I did this for days which turned into weeks. I would not finish the project.

After Mom's death, I did not cry as much as I was expected to. I discovered that there is an unwritten amount of grief the orphan is supposed to display, that there is grace in the throwing of arms around friends and sobbing on their shoulders at the mention of my mother. Losing Mom made me the recipient of unwanted sympathy, words of encouragement and ideas on how to deal with grief. I wanted to say, I'm not crying, can't you see? I'm okay, I don't need anything from you. I don't need you. I need mom. I need my Mom.

I spent my nights lying awake in bed, holding my husband's hand under the sheets and imagining that I was holding hands with Mom instead. Sometimes I curled up against his firm body and with eyes closed I sniffed that snug little nook on his chest and somehow it smelled of onions and tomatoes, of cows' brains, of bone soup and watery passion fruit juice. My husband smelled like Mom and in my dreams, she would rock back and forth in that chair that we got her for her last Mother's Day, but the moment I got close to her, the minute I bent over to kiss her forehead, she became my husband. The next morning I laughed at my nighttime fantasies, made more coffee than the day before, sat at the computer and stared blankly at the screen. For hours. I looked out of the window. There was a kingfisher sitting on our dock; he had a silvery something flapping in his beak. I ran inside looking for my camera. By the time I came back to the lake the bird was gone. Gone. Like Mom.

We are self-centered brats when we grieve. And this sentiment is so relentlessly true that nobody wants to accept it. When we grieve, we expect everybody to become malleable, to retreat from and to rush back into our lives on request. We expect to be excused from our responsibilities because we are busy dwelling on ourselves. Grief is the ultimate form of self-indulgence. My literary agent, upon hearing the news about the death of my mother, told me that she completely understood what I was going through because she had lost a close friend a few months prior. A friend? How could she possibly compare her grief to mine? Losing a friend is not the same as losing one's mother. My loss, I reasoned, had more weight than hers. This realization filled me with shame and made me weep in violent outbursts that rippled through me like jolts of electricity.

I tried to blackmail myself into going back to the research. I clipped Carlitos' picture to one side of the laptop. I forced myself to stare at his limbless body. I conjured the sound of his laughter, of Francisca cooing into his face, of the plastic apparatus fastened around his torso to keep him from tipping over. I thought about Esperanza's dead baby. I imagined her grave, her decayed little body, chunks of her whisked up in the air by desert vultures. I wondered which pain was worse, losing my mother or losing my own child. The former pain was unbearable, the latter inconceivable.

Writing while in mourning has a value of its own. It is not mere tears and longing and despair and the temptation to use writing as a cathartic placebo; it is something it took me a few years to welcome, to cultivate, to use and, in a way, to enjoy.

After a couple of two very near misses, my agent stopped sending the proposal to potential editors, and then she stopped being my agent. It wasn't Mom's death that brought my project to a screeching halt. It was my inability to honor the undocumented women who so openly shared their stories with me. I was left with the number one rule of writing: stick to what you know. And what I knew was my own life, shards of Mom's, some real, some imagined, and memories from my homeland, Colombia: a country that in memory never changes, a country I can't go back to because it exists only in a corner of my heart. It was only after my manuscript about Mom had been accepted for publication that I dared turn my attention again to the undocumented women. It would be fair to say that mourning's rude edges were softened and humanized by the subtle grace of acceptance. I'm still in mourning but I have given my grief a distinct and honored place in my writing.

I don't know where Esperanza or the other women are now. They could have migrated, died or been deported. I don't know. But they live in the stories they left behind, stories that smell of tortillas and *salsas picosas*. Stories told with defiance, with fearlessness, with hope, with humor. Stories about their *chinga* lives in this *chinga* country.

It is my hope that these women's words are read the way they were told to me: with their throats and their knuckles, with their wrists and their hearts, with rage and fire and love. It is also my hope that maybe one day I'll get the chance to see them again in a better place where they are no longer faceless wetbacks, but women. Like me.

Until then, *órale*, sisters.

About the Author

ADRIANA PÁRAMO is a nonfiction writer born and raised in Colombia.

After spending ten years in the oil industry as a student and as a petroleum engineer with a multinational oil company, she decided to leave her homeland and moved to Alaska. In 1996 she graduated from the University of Alaska Anchorage as a cultural anthropologist. There, she conducted an ethnochoreology among Yup'ik Eskimos, an innovative approach that linked their dances to their socio-cultural experiences.

Adriana later moved to Kuwait where she taught various subjects to young Muslim girls at a private school. There, she also engaged in advocacy of immigrant women's rights, specifically, Indian women working as servants. She designed a tool to assess the Quality Of Life of this group of immigrants whom she found living in squalor in one of the wealthiest countries in the world. The results of her fieldwork, along with explorations of the lives of other more privileged women living in Kuwait, evolved into *Desert Butterflies,* an unpublished manuscript.

After four years of research in the Middle East, Adriana returned to the USA. She taught Humanities and Anthropology at a college in Central Florida. Inspired by a story about an immigrant mother who walked the desert from Mexico to the USA with the dead body of her baby strapped to her own, Adriana immersed herself in the underground world of undocumented women toiling in the Florida fields. This fieldwork and the anonymous voices of the women she encountered while looking for the mother in the story are captured in *Looking for Esperanza*, winner of the 2011 Social Justice and Equality Award in creative nonfiction.

She is the author of *My Mother's Funeral,* (CavanKerry Press) which tells the story of a Colombian family of six women struggling to triumph among poverty and neglect. Interspersed between these stories are short snippets of the present life of the author, now an immigrant in the USA.

Adriana volunteered her time as a transcriber for *Voice of Witness*, a non-profit book series founded by author Dave Eggers, which empowers those most closely affected by contemporary social injustice. She co-produces *LOL, Life Out Loud,* the only reading series in Tampa Bay exclusively dedicated to nonfiction.

Her nonfiction work has been published in *CONSEQUENCE Magazine, Alaska Quarterly Review, So to Speak Journal, The Los Angeles Review, Fourteen Hills, Carolina Quarterly Review, Magnolia Journal, 580 Split, Phati'tude Literary Magazine, South Loop Review, New Plains Review, Compass Rose,* and *Concho River Review.*

She can be contacted at: www.paramoadriana.com

About Benu Press

Benu Press is a small, independent press committed to publishing poetry, fiction, and creative non-fiction. We believe in the transformative power of literature. To that end, we seek to publish inspiring and thought-provoking books about the practical dimensions of social justice and equity.

Published by Benu Press

Looking for Esperanza, Adriana Páramo
March on Milwaukee: A Memoir of the Open Housing Protests (script),
Margaret Rozga
Language is Power, Stephanie Reid
Confederate Streets, Erin Tocknell
Though I Haven't Been to Baghdad, Margaret Rozga
Love Rise Up, edited by Steve Fellner and Phil E. Young
High Notes, Lois Roma-Deeley
Two Hundred Nights and One Day, Margaret Rozga
All Screwed Up, Steve Fellner

For more information: http://www.benupress.com